BETTER MANAGERS
= BETTER BUSINESS

A contemporary approach to developing people managers

By Pete Fullard

ISBN: 9798687922890

For some great extra stuff go to www.bmbb.online

Table of Contents

Foreword by Roger Macey

Roger started his career in the mid-1950s as a management trainee at Ford Motor Company. After a stint as senior sales training lecturer at the Ford Marketing Institute, he left the company to become a Ford dealer. From a single franchise with a couple of outlets, he built a multi-franchise dealer group with a large number of outlets. He then left the corporate world and over the next 20 years, set up and sold several businesses in the motor finance and leasing sector. During this time, he became Chairman of the BVRLA, the retail motor industry trade body and then ECATRA, the European equivalent. He is a fellow of the Institute of Directors. After 'retiring' in the 1990s, he met Peter Fullard and became the initial investor in Upskill People. He has stayed with the company and is now non-executive Chairman.

We're often told that the workforce is changing, and that's true. The Millennials and Generation Zs now entering the workplace have different hopes and expectations to their parents. And their parents before them. But as someone who worked with some of today's youngsters' grandparents, I know the workforce has always been changing.

In a career spanning 60-odd years, I've worked with every generation currently on the planet, as well as some others who are long gone! So, I know how successive generations are shaped by their particular history, and by different kinds of upbringing, different cultural mores and different economic realities. Those who grew up with rationing and looked forward above all to a steady job for life, seem a world away from those who have grown up with the internet and aspire to a career that provides variety, emotional fulfilment and opportunities for growth. But then people have always found meaning and a sense of identity in their work. What's changed is how they find those things, and how that shapes their working lives.

If they are to get the most from them, employers need to understand what motivates their people. And part of that is understanding how upcoming generations differ from those who came before them. But an even bigger part of it is understanding what they have in common. Because some things don't change.

Technology changes year on year and decade on decade. Politics is constantly throwing up new uncertainties, both nationally and internationally. But fundamentally, people do not change. They want to contribute to their communities and their societies by working hard, gaining a sense of achievement in the process. They want that work to be fairly rewarded. And they want it to be recognised. Successful managers throughout the generations have understood this. They have 'got' people and how to motivate them to give their best. Those motivations change over time, but the fundamental need for recognition and reward does not.

A decent manager is one who understands that a business is only as good as its people, and that even the best people will only fulfil their potential if they are managed properly. A great manager is one who knows what that means in any given time and place - and for any given generation. They can also recognise that we all have a level at which we peak and above which we find ourselves out of our depth. We can't all be the boss, after all. In the past, I have seen this used against a manager's best interests. They are promoted to fail or remove them from the scene. That is not good management. That is an admission of laziness, and an abuse of power. You need to be able to spot if such practices are going on in your business and move to eradicate them.

Today's managers have to be everything the best of yesterday's managers were. They must understand strategy and know how to implement it at every level of their organisation. They have to be able to lead, to inspire and to coax the very best from their people. But to do that, they also must be able to empathise with a generation that sees work very differently from yesterday's workforce. To do that, they must be guides as much as leaders, mentors as much as bosses, listeners as much as speech-givers.

There are several specific challenges for those responsible for cultivating managers for the 2020s. The age of periodic training and annual appraisals is giving way to one of cyclical upskilling and continuous assessment and feedback. But fundamentally, the secret of success remains the same as always. Understand people, find out what makes your people tick, and never let go of the human touch.

This book is packed full of practical ideas for learning and development (L&D), who are usually part of the HR team, but equally as valuable for business owners and leaders. They all need to understand the concept to work in unison with L&D teams to upskill managers, and most importantly, know it's working.

Before we start

Why I wrote this book

Over a quarter of a century, I've worked with hundreds of business leaders who simply wanted their managers to be able to deal with challenges, take advantage of opportunities and increase performance. Their managers wanted to do those things too. But, somehow, things just weren't clicking into place. Managers ended up doing and not delegating, and certainly not implementing the business strategy. And despite their best efforts to rise to the challenge by investing in learning and development (L&D), business leaders were even more frustrated by the seeming impossibility of measuring the impact of that investment.

That's why I wrote this book, to unlock potential and help people shine. It started with four years' intensive research and development that my fabulous colleagues and I put into a series of online learning courses called Managing People. They evolved into a whole approach that's working really well in addressing the issues described above. We know that because we measured the results.

We faced a lot of challenges, generated a lot of perspiration and enjoyed a lot of inspiration, but we came up with a lot of innovative ideas, some of which proved incredibly effective. In the chapters that follow, I'm going to set out what I've learned, and show how a business of any size can upgrade its existing management development programme, to deliver better managers, who will deliver a better business, often saving money in the process.

Who did I write this book for? Well, on the face of it the obvious audience is the human resources (HR, or whatever else you choose to reference them as such as talent management; I prefer the latter but I'll stick with HR in this book as most people know what that is) or learning and development (L&D) people, but my intention was to make it of equal value to senior leaders, directors and business owners. There is one very simple reason for that: only when both sides understand each other, how they work, what they need and how they measure success, can they work in unison to create a continually improving group of managers. Some of the chapters that follow will also help senior people to define and clarify their goals, because great things can only be built on solid foundations. And giving people outside HR and L&D a concise insight into what the best L&D teams are doing allows senior managers to know what questions to ask, where to challenge and where to support.

Great businesses have great people and great people are those who are well managed. Great managers deliver the triple 'P' bottom line: people, planet, and of course, profit.

Best of all, the underlying principles I'll set out apply to any good learning, so you can use it all or just pick some ideas to enhance what you already have. As well as explaining the thinking behind each part of the approach, I'll give examples based on our implementation of each element, from measurement to personalised upskilling and continual support.

This is a very practical guide on developing people managers, it's also intended as a crash course for senior executives and business owners on the topic. While very few have any formal qualification in HR or L&D, most understand that it's a strategic investment worth taking seriously. I want to channel that positivity into some practical learning that will ensure those outside HR are better informed and more in tune with modern thinking on L&D. The reason for this is I believe they should take HR as seriously as they do finance, marketing or IT and for this to happen there must be more understanding, on both sides. People usually make the biggest difference in any organisation's performance.

At the same time, I want to help HR people understand how senior executives think, and how to engage Boards in their language to get behind learning and development that really makes a difference, and ties in with strategy, that can be truly and consistently measured. And let me warn you right now that it involves data! Over the years, far too many HR people have told me, "We don't do data". Well, you do now. Good learning is measurable, which means it's possible to demonstrate both progress and value for money. Most strikingly, the data often shows that it's possible to achieve more, with less time and money, by taking a contemporary approach and using some innovative thinking.

What I'm going to describe requires commitment from everyone. But once HR and L&D people are working together with decision makers or the Board, they can really make a difference, and fast. The key is communication. If you're really going to develop your people in line with the company's purpose, values and mission, everyone must be comfortable discussing them. And everyone must understand how the company's approach to L&D fits into its broader strategic goals. The first questions to ask are, do the HR and L&D people even know what those goals are? And are they truly on board?

Measure the outcomes

Aligning people and strategy is just the first step. The real leap forward comes when you learn to measure the outcomes of learning. If you're paying for delivery, whether in the form of digital, face-to-face or whatever, you'll get something delivered. But unless you measure the outcomes, you'll have no idea whether you're getting behaviour change and a meaningful return on your investment. What can your managers do after a course that they could not do before? How is learning and development changing the way they behave? Can you answer those questions for your business? Read on to find out how you can.

You've probably noticed something quite important. Most of your team carry a sophisticated little computer with them most of the time. They use it to keep in touch with friends, to organise their lives and as a source of entertainment. The younger ones - and many of the not-so-young ones - are on their phones so much that some employers consider them a nuisance. But what if they could be used to access learning, experts for coaching/mentoring and to measure what's been learnt? They can.

Bringing learning up-to-date means delivering it in a way that accords with the preferences and expectations of an increasingly millennial-dominated workforce. Doing it that way also makes it easier to measure outcomes.

Once you've defined your managers' competencies and how they need to behave, you're able to measure how they are improving - or not. I have seen that in the successful companies I've worked with, the best results come from an innovative blend of curated online resources and further support, such as virtual (and real) workshops, one-to-one coaching/mentoring and personalised continual development. Remembering to consider practicality, budget and any other constraints that must be worked around.

The principles are explained in the chapters to come, but the basic pattern of ongoing assessment and improvement can be summarised as follows:

- Define what you need your managers to be able to do
- Assess current ability level
- Create a learning programme
- Provide knowledge and convert to skills
- Enable further support to entrench behaviour change
- Assess ability level
- Review, revise, repeat

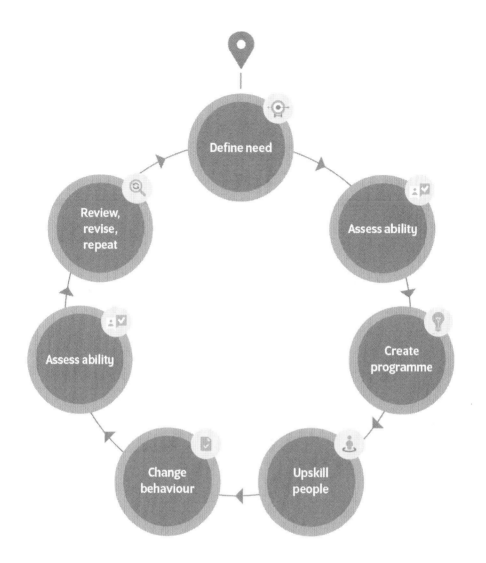

If you need to cultivate managers who really will transform your business, read on. Each of the chapters includes practical advice and a checklist so you can be sure you have what you need to make progress. When you can check them all off with confidence, you'll be well on your way to making better managers and a better business.

Chapter 1 - Aligning people and strategy

Sense of purpose

Any successful business needs to have a clear sense of purpose. Unless everyone knows what the company is there for, there's little chance they'll contribute to its success beyond following process (sometimes!). And even if they can recite a mission statement, unless they have a clear idea of what their own role is and what they will be judged on, even their best efforts could be misdirected. It's up to managers to ensure their teams not only know what they are doing and how to do it, but are motivated to do it well. And ultimately, it's up to senior management and directors to ensure their managers are adequately coached to play that role.

Now, before you read further and start to wonder what all this has to do with developing managers, there's a very important point to consider. Business managers should have an idea where they are going with the business and how they plan to succeed. This is their strategy and it can take many forms. They will ensure everything is in place to maintain good corporate governance, complying with rules to operate safely and inside the law, but their focus will mainly be on things that help them achieve success. Anything that isn't directly linked to strategy will naturally not get the highest priority (if any priority at all), after all it's often said, "What gets measured gets done" and it's usually true. HR and L&D teams are rightly focused on people, and the majority want the very best for their colleagues and know that great people are at the centre of a great business. However, to get the full backing of the Board (and the necessary investment of time, money and resources) they need not only to understand the business strategy but also to align their activities with it. That means recruiting and upskilling people to have the right skills at the right time for the business. Business leaders also need to recognise how their managers need to behave to deliver the strategy, and then work in unison with HR and L&D to make sure they have the skills to do it.

All good business leaders would agree they must have a strategy, so none of this is news, of course. From best-selling business guru Simon Sinek's 'start with why' to management legend Andy Grove's 'objectives and key results', or OKRs, the importance of having a clear purpose and specific goals is a part of conventional business wisdom. You need to know what your business exists to achieve, and how you are going to measure progress from day to day and month to month.

Having a clear strategy is not the whole story. Even the most visionary business leaders sometimes struggle to communicate clearly and consistently. Many failed strategies fail not because they are flawed, but because they are poorly communicated. The Chief Executive Officer (CEO or Managing Director) might have explained a brilliant strategy and got the backing of the Board, but unless they can get their managers on board, and ensure those managers are capable of implementing that strategy through all the people in an organisation, it'll never be more than a great idea. So, are your managers communicating your strategy, living and breathing it, throughout your business?

Poor communication does not always mean a simple lack of communication, it's the quality of it. As Dunning Kruger said in his TED Talk, "When talking to an idiot, make sure they are not doing the same". A survey for the Harvard Business Review found that nearly 90% of middle managers believe their bosses are communicating their company's strategy frequently enough, but it turns out frequency is not the point. Issues arise when we measure the wrong things. In this case, executives tend to measure communication in terms of inputs - emails sent, meetings convened - rather than outcomes. Do people understand the strategy and their role in it? In fact, only 55% of middle managers in the survey could name even one of their company's top five priorities. How many of yours can do that?

Another thing to be concerned about is having too many priorities to focus on. Middle managers are four times more likely to blame an excessive number of corporate priorities and strategic initiatives for getting in the way of implementing that strategy, than they were to blame a lack of clarity in communication. You can send all the emails you like and have all the workshops delivered in crystal clear language, but if the strategy itself is complicated or confused, it's not going to stick. And what's the one thing guaranteed to make things even worse? Nearly a quarter of middle managers complain that top executives keep changing their messages.

A further challenge is that we often use different words to mean the same thing. Or indeed the same word to mean different things! Look at most companies' websites and you'll find a vision or mission statement, usually there will be a purpose too. Oh, and some values. And in too many cases, they will be more or less interchangeable.

More clear-sighted businesses will distinguish between their purpose, mission (or vision) and values. Mission generally means what the organisation does and for whom, it can arguably be interchanged with vision. I'm going to stick with just purpose, mission and values. There are numerous definitions of these three words, so I'll set mine out now.

Purpose is why the organisation exists and what it's here to do. The mission is where the organisation is going right now, what it looks like in the future. This may change, sometimes subtly, sometimes quite significantly. Upskill People's purpose is 'To help people shine'. Upskill People's mission is 'To be the first choice for measurable learning'.

Values have more to do with how you go about things, Upskill People's team are all about 'Understanding, innovating and delivering on our promises, all with integrity and commitment'.

One key question is what might be open to change and what's not? The purpose of a company, the reason it was founded and continues to exist, is unlikely to change. A mission might change with the business landscape or new technology, or indeed once a previous mission has been achieved. For example, Tesla changed one word in their mission statement that made a big difference, they went from 'To accelerate the world's transition to sustainable transport', to 'To accelerate the world's transition to sustainable energy'.

Whatever your purpose, mission and values, it's essential that you take your people with you. If your business is successful, it's because your managers and their teams are aligned with the existing business strategy. If that changes, they need to know about it. More than that, they need help to develop or acquire the knowledge and skills required to make the new strategy succeed. That means you all need a clear understanding of what exactly they need to know and what exactly they must be able to do. This should be where learning and development comes in.

The key to managing change, and indeed to maintaining success over the long term, is to have a clear sense of purpose pervading every part of the company, including learning and development. And whether you call it your core purpose, your mission statement, the vision thing or anything else, it's essential that everyone understands how the company will pursue that end. And that brings us to strategic themes, objectives and key results (OKRs), 'moon shots', 'spotlights' and 'big rocks'. Simply put, the stuff you need to achieve. But, first, a word on those values before we look at objectives.

Values and the triple 'P'

Values can often look like a cosmetic add-on to a company's real purpose. We all know we have to care about the environment (the planet in the triple 'P' bottom line), about diversity and inclusion, about peace and love. Beyond that, smart business leaders understand that values genuinely matter, not only because it's important to be a decent human being, but also because they're good for business. Direction comes from directors and they must lead by example, truly living the values, all the time.

There are also alternative approaches such as Redcliffe who uses three elements. Future - define the future state of the organisation, the vision, but with mission and purpose wrapped up inside. Engage - the whole organisation in a way that individuals buy-in and appropriate that future to make it their own vision (not just the boss's). Deliver - ensure the means (human, resources, training, financial, processes, strategy, etc.) so that the organisation can realise the future. Whatever approach you chose the main thing is to have one, define it, and make sure everyone understands it.

Regardless of your approach or what you use to describe why you're here, a key value I'd urge all business leaders to take to heart is empathy - understand the organisation's personality. This is part of the wider topic of emotional intelligence (known as EQ), where IQ is intelligence quotient, a score from a standardised test, to assess an individual's intelligence, but in the context of business. Business empathy allows dialogue to flourish between all members of a team, which helps establish an atmosphere of trust and foster an environment in which people genuinely want to work. And empathetic management begins by making sure the company's other values are shared by everyone. They should inform recruitment as well as ongoing development. That's because before everyone at a company can be fully on board with its strategy, they must share its values.

So called 'value incongruence' occurs when people, especially managers, are not aligned with their company's values. For example, someone with a strong sense of responsibility to the environment will not fit in well at a company whose ruthless pursuit of profit causes pollution. People who aren't your type of people will become stressed, unhappy and less productive, and that's not good for anyone.

Wellbeing

The wider issue of wellbeing is increasingly recognised as being essential to support continued business success. Recent studies show as much as 40% of long-term absence from work is down to mental health issues and poor mental resilience. Managers are the key to supporting your people's wellbeing. They need skills and an understanding of the right approach to keep their team well, and most importantly motivated to be on the company mission.

That's why employers are increasingly recognising the importance of promoting wellbeing at work. Moreover, it's increasingly clear that the way people are managed is key to their wellbeing. Effective managers need to have the knowledge and skills to keep their people engaged, happy and flourishing. Do your managers have the knowledge and skills they need?

The good news is that there are trailblazers to emulate, companies whose Boards work in unison with L&D and HR to recruit, manage and develop the best talent. Those organisations have complete belief in the strategic direction of the business and the culture in which people will flourish. Crucially, they also understand the different aspirations and expectations of the generation now beginning to dominate the workplace. Millennials want coaches rather than bosses, and continuing dialogue rather than stodgy annual reviews. Smart businesses can both meet those expectations and get more from their people.

When everyone at a business is aligned in terms of values, and when L&D teams are brought on board with the C-suite's (CEO, CFO, CPO, etc.) strategy, the real magic can begin.

A business with a clear purpose and a defined strategy can identify themes, perhaps five to seven priorities to focus on at any given time. Sometimes these are known as the company's 'big rocks' - challenging but achievable goals for the short to medium term. It's important not to have too many. Bill Gates and Warren Buffett famously agreed that sometimes the key thing in business is deciding 'what not to do' rather than 'what to do'. A refined set of priorities allows everyone to keep their eyes on the prize, and to know that every minute spent chipping away at one of the company's big rocks is a minute well spent.

It's all about focus, and this is the thinking behind the objectives and key results approach (OKRs), where every manager and team member knows what they are expected to do and how their achievements will be measured. And the beauty of this approach is that it allows organisations to identify the particular manager competencies that are essential at any given time, for now and the near future. These will invariably include some of the competencies good managers already have, but clarity on this allows for a focus on ensuring everyone's skills in that area are good enough now. If they aren't, then the development programme can be adapted to focus on these.

Just as an ability to repeat the company's mission statement is no guarantee that someone is aligned with its strategy, a theoretical understanding of what needs to be done to further that strategy will not necessarily equip a manager with the ability to succeed. Knowledge is not the same as a skill, and even having a skill is not the same as using it on a day to day basis.

Really effective learning does not just convey ideas. It promotes a change to consistent and correct behaviour. This is where a more sophisticated approach to learning is required. One that considers how people learn, and how people of distinct generations and from different cultures learn differently, as we'll see later. And, once again, it starts with measurement - the subject of the next chapter.

Aligning people and strategy: Checklist

Start with a clear purpose and strategy

This one is for directors, leaders and business owners. If you don't know what your business is aiming for, and why, you're never going to be able to get your people on board. And you need more than a mission statement: you need clarity in what you need to achieve and how, one that's simple enough for everyone to understand but ambitious enough to capture everyone's imagination. Ask your people what they tell others they do for a living and what the team/environment/vibe is like? Does their answer capture what the business means to you? Are your purpose/mission/values unique to you or vague and ambiguous like other organisations?

Know your strategic themes

Strategic themes, 'big rocks' or objectives and key results (OKRs) are what connect your business strategy to your day to day activity. The clearer they are, and the better your people understand them, the greater your chances of achieving your medium to long-term goals. It's also important to be clear about what's not a priority at any given time, so people are investing their time appropriately. Tell your people how they fit into the business, what's expected of them and, crucially, how their performance will be measured and reported back, objectively and subjectively. One other thing to remember, when your measurement shows success, don't forget to celebrate it.

Base your management development on your objectives

Learning and development is not something you can do in isolation from the business strategy. You don't just need average managers demonstrating an adequate level in the competencies you specify; you need managers truly capable of implementing your strategy. So, map a list of the key management behaviours needed to realise your strategy and check your managers have them. A quote attributed to several people from Edison to Einstein is spot on here, "Vision without execution is just hallucination."

Live your values

It's essential that your people share your organisation's values. Value incongruence - a mismatch between what the company stands for and what its people believe in - is a recipe for discontent, demotivation and unsatisfactory performance. So, make sure you recruit and retain people who actually want to be there. And, on that note, put empathy at the heart of how you manage your people. Ask your people how the company's values are reflected in their day to day work, and keep checking.

Understand your people's needs and expectations

Good people are not blank slates. They come with needs and expectations of their own, and those needs and expectations change over time and from generation to generation. If you want to align them with your business, you need to understand what makes them tick, what motivates and inspires them. As is increasingly likely, if your people are Millennials (or Generation Zs), you need to understand that isn't always a job for life and a simple career path. A key management skill is the ability to get different personalities working together, and to have difficult conversations when necessary. Ask your people how you can help them help their teams to shine.

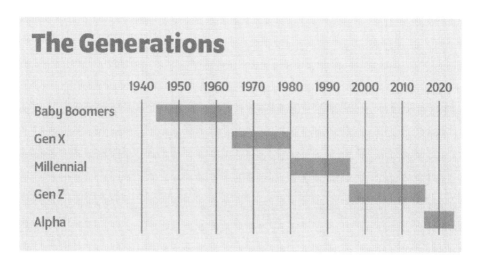

So, what are you thinking?

Now's a good time to reflect and note any ideas you have...

Chapter 2 - Mapping competencies and more

Managers who fit

A business with a clear purpose and well-defined strategy depends on managers who understand where they fit into that strategy. More than that, they must be capable of doing what is required of them. The key to your strategy's success is managers with the particular skills, attitudes and habits of behaviour necessary to play their part in making the strategy happen.

Knowledge on its own is only the start. Knowing has to be converted into skill. And even having the skill to do something won't help if someone simply isn't motivated to do it, is not in the habit of doing it, or if their every instinct says they should be doing something else. And, bear in mind, these could be perfectly good instincts, honed over many years in a successful management career. It's just that they're not aligned with the company's strategy here and now. What's more, it's hardwired into many of us to resist change, because we are afraid of risk and uncertainty. So, do your managers have the right stuff to play the role you need them to play, not when you hired them (or last upskilled them), but right now? If not, how can you help them develop and adapt?

First, as discussed in the previous chapter, you need to identify the competencies and behaviours your managers need in order to do what you need them to do. Accurate and up-to-date job descriptions are a good start, setting out what's required for the role in line with the business and the type of person, including their values. So, assuming you've got the right type of people, how do you assess whether your managers have what it takes to meet those job descriptions?

It's essential to be able to break a management role down into specific competencies. I and the team at Upskill People identified seven key competencies that underpin good management. These are: team working, communication, adapting to change, relationships, planning and organising, ability to analyse, and delivering results.

Then we identified specific behaviours associated with each competency, 69 in all. For example, two behaviours associated with the competency 'adapting to change' are: 'Questions why things are being done; doesn't just follow past practice' and 'Proactively suggests improvements to processes, systems and services; commitment to continuous improvement'.

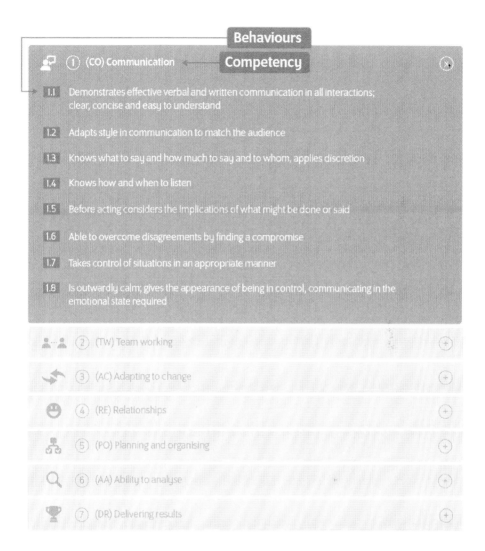

You can download the full set of competencies and behaviours at www.bmbb.online

Another question to ask is which behaviours are most relevant to a company's strategy at any given time? If you can answer that, you can tailor your development activity to the company's current needs. To that end, you need to be able to assess whether your managers have those competencies and behave in practice the way you need them to, both individually and collectively.

There are lots of approaches to assessing managers' abilities, one of the most well-known is 360 feedback, which collates opinions from a variety of sources including peers, direct reports, more senior colleagues and customers. 360 feedback has the benefit of being comprehensive and combining a variety of perspectives rather than just one, though it might be more accurate to describe it as an aggregate of subjective views rather than something completely objective. It also relies on each participant being skilled in assessing and giving feedback, and having no bias. The downside is that 360 feedback is, by its nature, time consuming and often expensive to do well, which means it's a challenge to be able to do it regularly enough to keep track of your managers, especially as their teams change and they move around.

Employee engagement surveys can also give an insight. The perspective they give is not definitive, but it's certainly part of the picture, and should not be discounted. Again, frequency can be a challenge, as it takes time to analyse the data to give a consistent and accurate view that managers can act upon with confidence.

Obviously, technology solutions can help here, especially those that report in real time. Then it's possible to instantly analyse the data and decide what is company-wide that can't be addressed (and acknowledged to the team), what is company-wide and can be addressed (act on it and tell the employees what you're going to do and when) and what is limited by specific demographics, job roles, departments or geography (then act on this in a targeted way). Then a subset of the entire group (20% for example) can be surveyed again to measure impact after shorter periods, such as three months, if not more often, even weekly 'reflections' or 'insights'. Measuring the 'pulse' of your people often can give some invaluable insights. Again, this progress and impact can be reported back to the team.

Quick enough, good enough

While in-depth gathering and the analysis of the data can be very useful, it's debateable whether it's quick enough, cost effective and consistent (being subjective if people's views are involved). 'Good enough' can be done ever more cost-effectively and quickly, providing there's enough information to act smartly, for example via an online skills check.

So, what does an effective quick check of skills look like? It might be easiest to start by saying what it doesn't look like. It doesn't look like the kind of 'multiple guess' quiz too often used to assess people after conventional group teaching. Anyone who has been on a few away days (face-to-face or virtual) or experienced all-too-common 'old style' online training courses, will be familiar with quizzes where you could have guessed the correct answers even before the course itself - if only because they stand out from the lazily put together wrong answers by virtue of being longer! In any case, when the purpose of the quiz is simply to confirm that several people have successfully completed the course, perhaps by copying someone else's answers, it's of very limited value.

The more profound limitation is that traditional metrics for assessing learning are one dimensional. Did they pass? If so, tick the box and move on, regardless of whether they learned anything useful they can implement. At best, such assessments are too simplistic.

The key difference with effective quizzes is that the results are actually meant to be looked at and taken seriously. You don't just want to know if people 'passed' or 'failed'. You want to know which questions they got right and which they got wrong, so that you can personalise the analysis by individual, team, all the way through to the whole company.

By designing well thought out scenario-based assessments, asking people what they would do in realistic situations, you can gauge not only where they might be going wrong, but how they're going wrong.

The most sophisticated scenario-based assessments should be challenging. This means the manager picking from a number of courses of action, and then deciding which combination is right and sometimes in what order. It doesn't take too many questions to gain a lot of information. With as few as 10 well-written questions, a sophisticated and revealing assessment can be completed in under 30 minutes.

And of course, the beauty of quick quizzes, especially when made available online, is that they are easily repeatable and can be done at any time on any device. Being online, it's also at near zero cost to deliver, administer and analyse in real time.

Here's an example from Upskill People's 'Quick Skills Check' online assessment which is part of the Managing People series.

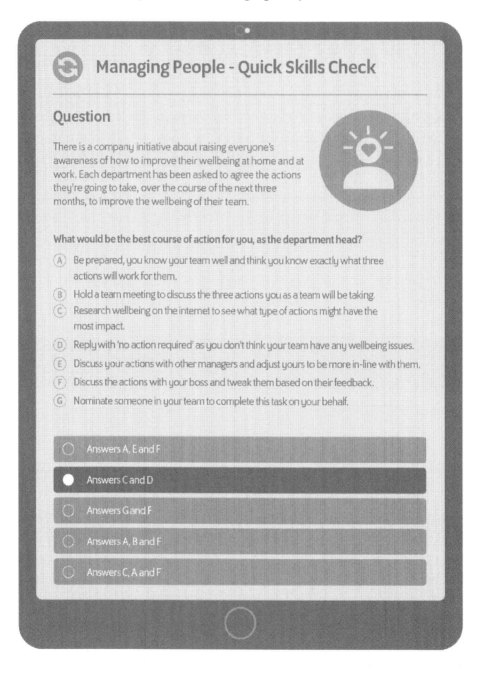

Managing People - Quick Skills Check

Question

There is a company initiative about raising everyone's awareness of how to improve their wellbeing at home and at work. Each department has been asked to agree the actions they're going to take, over the course of the next three months, to improve the wellbeing of their team.

What would be the best course of action for you, as the department head?

(A) Be prepared, you know your team well and think you know exactly what three actions will work for them.

(B) Hold a team meeting to discuss the three actions you as a team will be taking.

(C) Research wellbeing on the internet to see what type of actions might have the most impact.

(D) Reply with 'no action required' as you don't think your team have any wellbeing issues.

(E) Discuss your actions with other managers and adjust yours to be more in-line with them.

(F) Discuss the actions with your boss and tweak them based on their feedback.

(G) Nominate someone in your team to complete this task on your behalf.

- ○ Answers A, E and F
- ● Answers C and D
- ○ Answers G and F
- ○ Answers A, B and F
- ○ Answers C, A and F

Clients have used this to direct their efforts and to demonstrate to the Board when management development is needed to deliver the strategy. It's one of many inputs to use in defining what the programme should achieve and what should be included. The same idea can be used at a more advanced level to gauge the progress made by managers after a course, as we'll discuss in the chapter on 'Knowing it's working' later.

In fact, quick and regular assessment is also more in line with the preferences of Millennials, who value frequent and more informal feedback over slow and bureaucratic forms of assessment. It allows for an encouraging 'thumbs up' where they are getting things right and flags any areas where they're struggling before things get too far behind. Best of all, it highlights the need for more and better learning before bad habits become entrenched. In that way, it promotes a 'virtuous circle' in which regular assessment drives skill development that is personalised to the individual's needs, leading to better results.

This multi-dimensional approach allows us to test more than knowledge. It gives a good sense of someone's ability to implement that knowledge as a skill, by considering attitudes and habits of behaviour. To give a simple example, it's easy for someone to remember that SMART objectives are Specific, Measurable, Attainable, Relevant and Time-Bound, but quite another to know what that means in practice and to have developed an aptitude for creating and using them, and knowing when to use them. A well-designed quiz should check that. One other thing, don't always look for the individual level of competence, look at the spread of levels of competence. You need a rounded and balanced set of skills for each and every manager. Clearly, we're all different and have things we're good at and things we'll always have to work on, but looking at shortfalls, individually and as teams, will help direct where you invest your development resource.

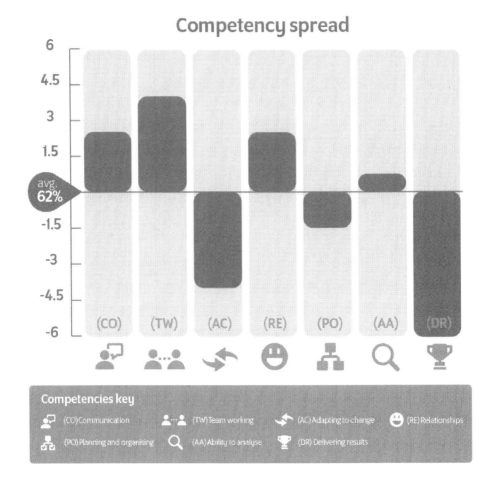

How are your managers behaving?

Having a great set of behaviours grouped into competencies allows you to measure the performance of every part of your management development programme. If any element of the programme doesn't improve on one of your defined behaviours, what's it doing in the programme?

Assessments aren't just for testing at the end of a course. You can make interactive, scenario-based testing much of the learning. Upskill People's Managing People courses, which we'll see examples of later, are each an episode containing two interactive continuous assessments, just like real-life, all linked to the mapped competencies. Content-rich, scenario-based assessments, broken down by question rather than pass-fail, allow for genuinely granular and qualitative measurement of someone's knowledge, skills and ability. That makes the resulting data worth something and can be acted upon. Not only 'completion rates' for each question, but also the time taken, and the average number of attempts can be captured and broken down demographically. That way you can identify patterns of performance among different functions, age cohorts, levels of seniority and geographical locations, allowing you to identify areas in need of attention, both people and programme content.

And of course, the same principles we've outlined above can be applied after managers have been developed, with assessments linked to specific elements of learning and analysis drawn from them. This indicates the progress made and, more importantly, helps in the continual calibrating of the company's management development in line with its strategy.

So, simply put, check it! Is your development programme working? Continuous testing is the only sure way to measure effectiveness and ensure what you and your team are doing is working for your business.

Mapping competencies and more: Checklist

Start with strategy

The key to assessing your people is a clear idea of your business strategy and the skills they need to support it now. A manager who is good at everything except what you actually need them to do, is not going to help your business succeed. And in addition to knowledge and skills, that means having the right attitude and behaviour. All those things can be learned, but only once you've identified the need for that learning. So, translate your strategy into the specific competencies that are important right now and then tell your people what those are. Work with them.

It doesn't have to be all or nothing

You can tell a lot from a quick quiz, provided it's carefully designed to tell you what you need to know. Scenario-based assessments can be completed online at the learner's own pace, so use them to quickly identify areas where someone is not yet where they need to be, and could use some support.

People like being measured!

It's true. Studies have shown that people who feel challenged at work are far more engaged and happier, and regular measurement is a key factor. People whose work is never measured or assessed, quickly become frustrated and fed up. Far better to have regular check-ups to identify areas for improvement, or simply provide feedback for good work, than to leave people in the dark or waiting for an annual review that has little bearing on their day to day work. So, check your people often, in a variety of ways and tell them how they're doing.

Focus on the design of assessments

Simply adding up passes and fails is a wasted opportunity when an assessment can also tell you so much more, such as specifically where and how your people are going right and wrong. If assessments are linked to your business mission you can use them to identify exactly how well aligned your people and strategy are. That way, assessment drives learning which drives performance, as we will see next.

So, what are you thinking?

Now's a good time to reflect and note any ideas you have...

Chapter 3 - Thinking strategically about learning

Your plan

Most businesses have a management development plan of one kind or another. But whether you have a dedicated department or a more informal approach across the business, there are three important questions:

- Is it aligned with the business strategy?

- Is it adequately skilled and resourced?

- Is it informed by systematic measurement of outcomes with reference to your strategic goals?

If you can answer those three questions, you'll be able to decide if your learning strategy is serving your people and working for your business as it should.

This chapter sets out some of the key considerations to bear in mind when developing a management learning strategy that's contemporary and delivers more value at less cost. That is assuming you're currently doing something to develop your managers. Doing nothing to make sure you have great managers will be costing you dearly every single day. There is no need to take a 'year zero' approach and start from scratch. Most of what we'll discuss can complement rather than replace what you already have. And much of it costs very little if anything at all, but delivers an immediate cost saving, especially over face-to-face training (real or virtual).

Focused learning

One important principle is to focus learning on those who will benefit most from it. In any business there are high-fliers who hardly need encouragement to develop and improve themselves. Help them how they need it, in a personalised and focused way, but let them get on with it. There may also be some who need help just to get to a basic standard, and provided the issue is not more fundamental, such as their values being incongruent with those of the organisation, you can provide that help. But it's important not to neglect those in the middle, which could be most of your managers. Steady improvement among this group will often have the greatest positive impact on overall organisational performance. With upskilling, it's important to personalise and offer choice so everyone gets what they need to achieve the level required.

Of course, your managers are far from being an undifferentiated mass, so it would be a mistake to treat them as such. Different people learn in different ways, so learning should be designed to accommodate all styles and approaches, rather than trying to force everyone to learn the same way.

First think of the particular role - and the competencies identified as being important for that role - and then to the particular individuals: experience, generation, culture and personality all make us wonderfully unique and that should be reflected in an accommodating learning design.

The science bit

There is a lot of science to draw on here to define and understand each other, but we can also use some common sense. The Myers-Briggs Type Indicator focuses on four separate dichotomies in our personalities: extroversion versus introversion, sensing versus intuition, thinking versus feeling and judging versus perceiving. Each combination of the four adds up to a personality type, and this underpins many of the personality tests you can find online today. Some, such as 16personalities.com, have taken this a little further and made it more approachable. It has an additional name for each type, such as Commander, Protagonist, Defender or Entertainer, and fleshes out the associated preferences and behaviours to help people understand themselves and one another. Then there's others like the 9-box approach, and linking personalities to colours. The list is very long, and each has its own merit.

Another is the Big Five personality traits. These have some overlaps with Myers-Briggs, but can be used in a more granular way, with individuals scored separately for each trait: openness to experience, conscientiousness, extroversion, agreeableness and neuroticism. It's also possible to identify demographic groups - men and women, people with different cultural backgrounds or professions - as being more or less likely to score highly for each trait. This is really a more rigorous way of thinking about something we all instinctively know - people are different!

However you choose to measure or analyse personalities, use them to help understand people but don't rely on them completely, people are nuanced. Be aware that we are all different, and that if we try to understand one another better, we can make allowances accordingly. Crucially, managers should not expect everyone in their team to work the same way they do and try to shape everyone around them in their own image. Far better to recognise and adapt to differences. A good manager will use their skills to see that one type of person is likely to be better suited to a role or task than another type of person, and vice versa. They'll know their people and use the resources they have in the best way. A little sensitivity to what makes each individual tick will make for a happier and more productive working environment for everyone. And when it comes to people development, it's important to let people also learn in a way that suits their personality.

In fact, there are also distinct styles of learning, which won't necessarily correspond to personality types, but make a huge difference to whether someone benefits from a piece of learning or not. Broadly speaking, there are visual and auditory learners, those who learn best by reading and writing, and even kinaesthetic learners, who prefer hands-on activities. If you can tailor someone's learning to their particular style, the results are likely to be that much better. One size does not fit all!

Another factor to bear in mind, especially if your business operates in more than one country or even continent, is cultural difference. Global consultants Hofstede Insights use a six-dimensional model to score different countries for different aspects of culture. The six dimensions are power distance (or acceptance of hierarchy), individualism, masculinity, uncertainty avoidance, long-term orientation (or the balance between past, present and future) and indulgence (as opposed to restraint). Erin Meyer, author of The Culture Map: Breaking Through the Invisible Boundaries of Global Business, goes two better than Hofstede's six dimensions with eight scales on her 'culture map'. These are communicating, evaluating, persuading, leading, deciding, trusting, disagreeing and scheduling, with a sliding scale for each between two extremes.

Whichever way you measure or analyse cultural difference, acknowledge and make allowances for it. This is particularly important when it comes to learning design at every stage, because people learn differently in different cultures, and the role of coaches and mentors will naturally differ in line with that too.

People in any culture also learn using a variety of media and can do so either on their own or by following a more formal course or curriculum. Self-motivated learners should of course be enabled to get on with reading books and articles, as well as watching videos, and to share insights with their peers, for example via a company social media group (internal or external).

More directed learning can make use of these resources too, especially by providing a carefully curated collection of reference texts, articles, factsheets and videos to focus learners on priority issues. And priority is a key word here. Just because the company happens to have a massive archive of PowerPoint presentations on this or that, does not mean they are worth asking people to spend time on. Regardless of the format, it's important to remember that time is money, and while learning people will not be doing other things which could be delivering bottom line benefits, and if they're being paid there'll be a salary cost. Nor is cheapness a reliable guide to what's economical. Small amounts spent on ineffective materials that are useless, or even demonstrating the wrong things, are small amounts wasted. And those add up to big amounts of time and money, all coming off the bottom line. The focus must stay on the operational needs of the business.

The company can also provide group face-to-face learning, whether physical or virtual. This has the great advantage of bringing people together, allowing for discussion and for people to learn at the same time as a group. This advantage is largely lost when classroom teaching is recorded for replay later, even with the ability to comment/discuss online.

But that can also be of value, as anyone who's been motivated or inspired by a TED talk or similar knows. It's all about quality.

You can also provide coaching and mentoring, which aren't the same thing, as we'll discuss in a later chapter. Coaching is a particularly valuable complement to other forms of learning. Properly understood, it's much more dynamic than conventional management 'training', which makes it that much more helpful when it comes to making learning stick and changing behaviour, as we'll see below.

The ideal learning environment

I have found that the ideal learning environment combines all the elements mentioned so far. Carefully curated, these different forms of learning complement and reinforce one another. When people come together in a face-to-face session, whether in real-life or online, it's incredibly helpful if people have already undergone a course of some kind in their own time, so they are all at the same level. It not only saves time, but it's vital for people who are new to the topic or certain personality types who like all the detail.

The following chapter sets out the 'how to' of putting together such a programme, but a strategic approach to learning requires the same careful planning at every stage as any other aspect of your business. So, be clear about the required outcomes, the skills and competencies you need your managers to master. About how you will measure success by building smart measurement into the learning. And about the scope of the project, including the budget and timescales. This is essential both to demonstrate that the learning will provide value for money and to avoid 'scope creep', which is when further elements, objectives and goals are added to the project as it progresses without considering the additional effort, costs and return.

Buy or build

Then the big decision is whether to buy or build elements of your management development programme. If it's already available it's quicker to buy and tailor, or add your own specific elements, especially for digital/online content. There are two big pitfalls I've repeatedly seen. The first is simply migrating classroom or printed materials online and calling it online learning. A great face-to-face management development programme doesn't make a great online learning programme - it's a completely different medium. The second is misjudging your internal L&D talent and their ability to design and build great online learning, for which they'll need the latest skills. As a result, many a project has failed to deliver and taken considerably longer than expected (and cost more), even when the inevitable corners are cut. There's also the danger of not allowing for ongoing review, maintenance and enhancement.

Internal teams are often tempted to not spend enough time listening and understanding the audience, researching best practice and then prototyping their ideas, especially those wonderfully enthusiastic and creative ones (who start well, but can fade fast and fail to get the job done well). They have time and budget constraints on each project, which can also limit their ability to keep themselves upskilled in the latest techniques and approaches. This is especially true of smaller internal teams, as organisations can become dependent on them and their knowledge, which is a business risk as they may leave or be unavailable for an extended period.

Good learning does not have to cost the Earth, and often it's possible to achieve a lot with a limited budget, especially when you utilise that great untapped creative resource - your workforce. There are often stars among them, and those who are great at being on camera, so go beyond the L&D team and their usual suppliers to make it your own. Often the materials produced by your own people connect with the others, even if they're a bit rough and ready.

The key is to be both strategic and agile: learning little and often can be more effective, and far more economical, than committing to a large-scale programme that can be hard to adapt or adjust in response to changing circumstances. Upskill People's Managing People series is the product of a steadily ongoing evolution and has undergone many iterations as the production team learned from all the feedback we received, the good the bad and the ugly! So, run a small-scale pilot scheme and learn the lessons before investing too much, too soon. All of this means you'll get there quickly and cost-effectively.

Thinking strategically about learning: Checklist

Focus help where it will do most good

Good learning helps people to fulfil their potential, and nearly everyone can benefit to some extent, but not all in the same way or to the same extent. People at different levels of ability and experience will benefit from more or less help accordingly. Take special care not to neglect the middling majority, their steady improvement will really make a difference to the business. So, identify priorities for maximum impact and spend wisely, use the Blue Ocean Strategy approach (created by W. Chan Kim and Renée Mauborgne), look for cost innovation alongside value innovation. Simply put, achieve more for less.

Make it personal

As much as possible, tailor the learning to your learners, focusing on their particular needs and potential. Different people learn in different ways, so factor in a variety of learning styles, for example by providing additional material for those who will benefit from it, and opportunities to discuss the learning with colleagues, so people can exchange notes with others who think and learn in the same way. Ask people for feedback on their learning materials and programmes.

Prioritise content

As we've discussed, learning needs to be aligned with your business strategy. Once you've decided which competencies you want to work on, make sure you weight your programme accordingly. If communication is a key priority, make sure the learning covers that. And don't let the proportions be skewed because you happen to have existing materials - if it's not relevant, leave it out!

Scope out the whole project in advance

Establish clearly defined objectives and parameters for the learning. Before you start developing a course, and especially before you start spending money on expensive media elements, such as animation/video/audio, make sure you are totally clear on the required outcomes, the budget and timescale, and how you will measure success and demonstrate value for money.

Aim for a blend of types of learning

Individual reading, online courses, group face-to-face learning, coaching and mentoring are all valuable. Online learning is often the most efficient and economical way for people to learn (if it's great quality), and crucially it lends itself to smart measurement. But it works best as part of a rich 'ecosystem' of learning, which will also help make the sum greater than the parts. Use different upskilling approaches to reinforce and complement one another.

Run a pilot to test your strategy

A small-scale pilot is the best way to check things are working as they should. So, start small, check and review the results, not only in terms of learning outcomes, but also value for money and time spent. Ask lots of questions and be good at listening and clarifying. The audience feedback is often the most useful, they are your customer. Understand before you innovate further and then deliver.

So, what are you thinking?

Now's a good time to reflect and note any ideas you have...

Chapter 4 - Using blended learning to make it stick

Effective content

We've already talked about the importance of being able to measure where your managers are and how they are progressing. The key to that is a clear understanding of what you need them to know, the skills you need them to develop and the behaviours you want to encourage and ingrain. This is also the starting point for designing effective course content.

A successful course is not one that ends with everyone walking away with a certificate - though it is a good idea to acknowledge their achievement. A successful course is one that equips managers with usable knowledge and skills that make them better able to do their jobs. It should also build their ability to understand and manage their own emotions, and those of the people around them, commonly known as emotional intelligence (or EQ).

The key to that is a clear idea of what the course's learning objectives are. Once you are clear about those objectives and measurable outcomes, it will be easier to define what should be included in your course - and what can be left out - so you can design content for your managers that really delivers. The same is true for any format of learning, whether online, face-to-face or virtual, be clear to begin with.

Indeed, the best learning will involve a blend of different elements - a curated reading list, video, interactive and group sessions, as well as coaching and mentoring, more of which later. But good blended learning is not just a bit of this and a bit of that. It brings together every element of learning at the right level and at the right time, to optimise the impact on the learner. The goal is not simply to convey information, but to change behaviour, so when and how learning is delivered is as important as what is delivered. For example, good online learning before face-to-face or virtual group learning is likely to optimise the impact of the latter, since everyone will have shared points of reference and understand the necessary base knowledge and key terms. They can then focus on role play and other ways of translating knowledge and skills into behaviours that stick.

Naturally though, good learning design begins with content. This chapter sets out the key principles behind any good online learning, even at a very basic level. You don't need a Hollywood budget to produce video that sticks in the mind, or Bollywood-style showcases to change the way people think and act. You just need a clear idea of what you want to get across and an understanding of how to make an impact. Great creativity and innovative thinking always succeeds.

Pick your platform

Before we look at content, a few words on the one essential thing you'll need. It's true you could use a platform like YouTube or Vimeo to distribute your content, but without proper individual learning road maps (or digital career paths), and performance data, you can't easily measure impact. Number of views doesn't really cut it. So, you need a learning platform of some sort. The most important thing is not to be taken in by something that looks wonderful and has lots of bells and whistles. I've seen a lot of systems where only a small amount of the functionality is actually used when bought and paid for, it becomes 'shelfware'. After all, how many of us use more than a small amount of what our word processor or phone can do? I've also seen some whose advertised functionality either isn't truly present ('vapourware'), doesn't quite work as advertised ('bleeding edge') or needs an IT team to configure and get the most out of it (user friendly only if the user is NASA!).

So, all I say is keep it simple, decide what you need and buy just that. Make sure it's easy to use and does what you need without lots of calls to the supplier support team. Also be certain if you do call, they will be there for you. It's often attractive to buy a learning platform as part of a wider 'enterprise', or 'people' system, but also consider a 'best of breed' approach for some elements. A good learning platform is open and should be easy to integrate, so find what you need, that will deliver the most bang for your buck, get a shortlist, and speak to other companies that are already using them.

Data to measure impact

Once you've got a learning platform to deliver the right stuff to the right people, and one that will give you all the data you need to measure what we're talking about, you should also consider one other thing. You need a tool that lets you build and publish courses. This should be very simple, one you don't need to relearn how to use every time you come back to do something a month later, or for that matter whenever a new upgrade is realised with yet more functionality you don't really need. It should be capable of putting your materials online and deploying assessments where the individual responses are stored and can be analysed later. It should also allow you to use your legacy content from previous projects and suppliers, if you have them, and gather post-course feedback for you to use to continually improve. When you're sure you've got those, then the fun can start in creating some behaviour changing online content.

Making an impact with learning content is about establishing an emotional connection with the learner. This is why video can be so powerful. For example, it's easy enough to stick a slogan on a slide that says, 'Effective communication is at the heart of good management', but if you really want people to take it to heart, you need empathy. It's far more effective to have a scene played out in which a manager is struggling to get through to someone or vice versa. The learning objective here is not simply for the learner to know that communication is important, but for them to internalise what it means in practice. Once they see how different approaches to communication have different results, they will really pay attention, because it's relevant to them and they understand that taking one approach over another will make a real difference.

This is nothing especially new. The best group learning uses role play to make the same kind of emotional connection, perhaps taking up as much as two thirds of time together. The danger with translating face-to-face workshop content to an online resource is a tendency to downplay the importance of emotion and empathy in favour of raw information. Of course, that information is important, the theory behind the best practice for communication in particular situations, and examples of the key words, acronyms and phrases everyone needs to know to follow the course. But spending 17 minutes of a 20 minute online course displaying text is a missed opportunity to make the most of the medium. Provide the content to be read, if it must be, but be sure to write it in plain language and explain why it's important. If it warrants the effort and is important enough, it'd be even better to bring it to life in scenarios and ideally video, so it's understood and retained. Remember to pause regularly to let things sink in, and always explain how to put new knowledge into practice as skills.

Going online should be seen as an opportunity to do things differently than you would in a face-to-face/virtual group or individual situation. There is no need to focus on the lowest common denominator as you might in a room full of people at different levels in terms of knowledge and skill. When the priority is bringing everyone up to the same basic level, the danger is that more advanced learners become disengaged and bored. Online, they can work at their own pace, in a good location, so they always feel challenged and learn something new. There is no need for everyone to spend the same amount of time on each piece of content. People with different learning styles and preferences can choose how they engage with the course. That's because the design is focused on the real purpose of online learning: not just to convey information, but to motivate, upskill and help people to change their behaviour and shine.

Real interactivity

We're talking about real interactivity here. It's a very overused word in online learning, but I mean realistic, challenging scenarios where people have to think - not 30 slides/pages with an occasional drag and drop (which isn't a good approach on mobile anyway). Rather than providing information and then testing learners on it, a truly interactive course challenges learners as they go by asking them to respond to realistic scenarios. Think of a situation in which managers must demonstrate a certain competency or way of behaving for example, knowing how to deal with a specific team member situation. Then illustrate that situation with true-to-life characters and ask the learner to choose between different courses of action and their timing. If they have the competency required, they will understand which option to take and why. If not, the course should feedback to help them understand, by providing the information and insights they need, and explaining how to apply these in practice.

I've found that people get more from dramatised, soap opera-style scenarios than from dry, fact-based presentations. These work when made up of a series of short (1-3 minute) video sections to get the point across quickly and easily. They should be realistic and true to life, including diverse characters so people can immediately see the relevance of what they're learning. A single scenario can focus on 3-4 skills over several stages and these are what's measured.

It's a great idea to have one of the characters set out the issues in an introductory clip, and to make text and graphics available to explain the skills necessary to meet the challenge. Ideally, learners should be able to read key points explaining what they need to understand, for example base knowledge and key terms, or to download optional documents/illustrations/infographics with more detail if they really want to dig down.

Interactivity then really comes into its own when learners are presented with a dramatic clip that leaves the protagonist with a decision to make, with genuinely meaningful choices. It's not a case of guessing the right answer just to get through the course, so much as learners asking themselves what they would do in a given situation. Once they've chosen, the best choice should be revealed and explained why it's the best answer. This is gradual learning, delivered just when it's needed. And this part is crucial, because management is not like arithmetic with clearly right and wrong answers, there are subtleties.

At any scenario decision point, where there are a number of options presented (at least three), it's always good to avoid the temptation of the silly or humorous wrong answer. It's better to design options where the poorest one will be picked by a percentage of the managers, so including one response that is understandable but not acceptable. This gives another opportunity to highlight how some behaviour, even if well motivated, isn't appropriate now (even if in previous times it may have been). Having another answer that is very good, and certainly acceptable, helps newer or less experienced managers build confidence (and we can't all make perfect decisions every time). This good but not best option causes more skilled managers to stop and think before selecting the correct one, that most accurately demonstrates the skills needed to get the best outcome. The course should always explain why as well as how, regardless of what's chosen.

Often the difference between the best answer and the second-best (or unacceptable) one is the difference between state-of-the-art management thinking and what used to be considered best practice. It's not that the old way of doing things is particularly bad, but more that it's a missed opportunity to do better. A learner who picks the best answer shows they are not only competent, but capable of getting the best from the situation and boosting performance in a way that is likely to lead to marginal gains, if not more.

This approach means learners are given detailed feedback in real time. And if they don't get the best answers, they can return to the part in the course where the skills are covered and replay the scenario again to help understanding, before discussing with their own manager or a coach/mentor anything they're finding particularly challenging. Best of all, it also means that measurability can be built into the learning. If questions are weighted according to the skill being tested, learners can be assessed not simply on the number of 'right' answers they get, but more importantly on the number of times they demonstrate each skill.

An immersive experience - Managing People

What I've described was the design approach for Upskill People's Managing People series of seven online courses and associated skills checks, an immersive learning experience. In successive episodes, the learner is introduced to a cast of characters, and they play the part of a manager facing various opportunities, dilemmas and challenges. Categorised under broad themes, they include wellbeing, recruitment, coaching and performance management. For example, in one '*Charlotte is carrying out reviews at Rise and Dine. A process made more challenging when performance issues get in the way, and team members raise serious concerns. Your role is to make the decisions that will help Charlotte navigate the reviews and make the right decisions when managing her team.'*

A great feature is that, having been through the courses, these characters and scenarios can be used as common reference points to be discussed among learners and between themselves and their managers or coaches. For example, faced with a real-life challenge involving performance issues, a learner will remember how Charlotte faced a similar situation, and immediately be reminded of the lessons learnt: 'What would Charlotte do?'

This is a good time to mention the 'g' word in online learning, I often hear people talk about having fun while learning through 'gamification'. I also hear some senior managers saying people are supposed to be learning not playing games and having fun! While well-written humour is a powerful tool, it's hard to truly pull off, unless you're using a skilled writer who truly understands the audience, and we all have a different sense of humour. A better word than 'gamification' is simply 'motivation'. The key element of playing games (especially software games) is to win or gather more credits/points and move to the next level. So, for me the real deal is in being challenged to get to the next level and achieve, rather than just testing the manual dexterity of someone's fingers to jump an obstacle or hit something.

We can look at an example from Managing People to illustrate this. After each pause in the storyline a decision point is reached and multiple options are presented, with around 10 decision points for each scenario. Just like real-life the situations are complex, so two or three wouldn't be enough. This is followed by feedback on the learner's decision where the best answer is explained, if they didn't pick it, along with signposted directions to the relevant knowledge. This gives learners a regular boost as they make their way through the course (if they get the answers right), or quickly highlights when they aren't quite where they should be, and need to digest the information a little more carefully, in the event they have skipped through a little too eagerly first time. Learners are then able to go back and read up on anything they're struggling to understand or apply in practice.

and I really wanna achieve
something here.

Current score: 93%

Key Skills

Motivate   Coach   Feedback   Monitor

Question 6 of 7

Oscar has talked a bit about why he wanted the chance to prove himself in the Team Leader role. How should Charlotte respond?

- **Option 1** - You really like working here and want to progress your career. Being promoted to Team Leader would feel like an achievement. You'd benefit from a pay rise, but it's really about proving something to yourself – is that a fair summary?

- **Option 2** - Here's a summary of what I've heard. You are motivated to work towards the Team Leader role, but at the moment you don't feel ready for it. Is that fair?

- **Option 3** - To summarise then, you looked up to Anna in the Team Leader role and thought 'I could do that'. The possibility of a pay rise is important to you, but at the moment you feel overwhelmed, and this is something we need to resolve.

However you organise your course, the key is to ensure all the content is completely relevant to the learner. By all means include additional content for those who may want it, this can be in the form of a video or simply a link to a PDF that explains something in more detail. But make a clear distinction between the core content that you expect all learners to absorb and take to heart, and bonus material for those who choose it. This approach works for those personalities who simply must have all the detail and understand the theory behind an approach - it's just the way they are, so accommodate them. If materials are well written most people will study them anyway. It also allows managers with more pragmatic personalities to grasp the essentials before progressing and developing their behaviour through practical implementation by working through the interactive scenarios. It's a way of building in personalisation and giving people choices and control.

For example, it's increasingly important for managers to have a good understanding of stress, mental resilience and other wellbeing issues that could affect them and their team. The learning outcome of a module on stress might be that everyone who passes should be able to recognise the signs of stress and know what to do about it for themselves and to help their team. But people with different personality types will want different levels of detail and background knowledge. For some, it will be useful to have a fact sheet or video explaining the science of stress: how our 'fight or flight' response kicks in when we perceive a threat, for example. Others will prefer a simple illustration of the signs of stress and clear guidance on how to support colleagues.

You can download some examples of linked documents at www.bmbb.online

There's no need to test people on the theory of stress. What you need to know is that they understand how the issue affects them, and what they should be capable of identifying and acting on in practical terms. That's why it's essential that the scenarios used are completely true to life in all its complexity.

Managing People's Wellbeing episode sets out four skills measured by 'batteries' required to deal with the issue, summarised in the acronym WELL: Watch, Engage, Listen, Lead. The video then introduces an employee who has taken on too much responsibility and is becoming overwhelmed. As a result, she is beginning to make mistakes and snap at colleagues. Her manager has to decide how to broach the issue sensitively to both improve the situation and protect the employee's wellbeing and mental resilience. A series of questions provide opportunities for the learner to demonstrate their grasp of the four WELL skills, thereby fleshing out exactly what they mean in practice.

Ideally, the learner will recognise the type of situation shown (such as an overworked and stressed employee) and immediately see the relevance of what they have learned. And when they encounter similar situations in future, they will immediately be reminded of that learning, we all remember 'stories'. These scenarios are also an invaluable point of reference for future coaching, as we will see in the next chapter.

So, effective learning needs to establish empathy about a character's predicament and then connect that feeling with an understanding of the solution. That way, the learner is not just absorbing information, but establishing an instinctive connection between a situation and the behaviour required to deal with it. This is how learning sticks and transforms behaviour for good. While online courses alone can't ever claim to change behaviour, they should deliver:

- Knowledge converted into skills

- The motivation to implement the skills and change behaviour

- The method to change behaviour, how to do it

If this is supplemented with further support to complement the learning, you have a great checklist for what everything that you buy (or build) should achieve.

Using blended learning to make it stick: Checklist

Start with the outcomes

Have a clear idea of what learners need to achieve and what they will be tested on. You can start with a big goal and break it down, work backwards from quiz questions to content and scenarios or a combination of both. Once you have the quiz, it'll show you what they need to know, then you can deliver it in the course and align the time spent on each topic with the questions that check them. This approach can really focus your design phase.

Get the script right

It's vital to get content right before going to production. For one thing, the cost of making changes rises exponentially as the process advances. So, tweak the objectives and outcomes first, and then the script, as much as it takes to get it right rather than risk having to reshoot photos/video, rerecord voice or revise animations/illustrations later. More importantly, a good script makes for a good course even if the production values are basic. Let the audience review the script and test a text-only prototype of the course, your build tool should make this easy and fast. Get writing!

Think emotional connection, not facts

The facts are easy to put on paper or on screen. Interactive learning is your opportunity to make the emotional connection that makes learning stick. Use relevant, realistic and real-life scenarios people will relate to, and characters they can identify with. The key is to establish empathy, so people feel the importance of what they're learning, rather than just absorbing the facts. For each scenario, decide how you want the learner to feel.

Know your audience

Good content is tailored to the audience, their learning style, culture, spoken language and role, so make sure it's right for your learners. That includes using the right tone and language. Literally, if your audience doesn't have English as a first language, you might even consider having the script or key words and phrases translated into other languages if that will make it easier for your managers. Adding closed captions/subtitles to video is easy and can really help improve understanding of video footage. Knowing your audience also means finding out what they do or don't like about group teaching, and what gets their attention. If in doubt, ask them!

Test it!

Once you have the key elements, learning outcomes, quiz and a script you're happy with, get as much feedback as possible, from some of the intended audience. Something that appeals to people in HR or L&D, or even to the Board, is not guaranteed to click with those intended to learn from it. So, seek their input throughout the process.

Know how you're going to measure it

The point of your course is to equip your people with usable knowledge and skills that make them better able to do their jobs. To that end, you need measurable learning outcomes, which should be woven into the course from start to finish. Whether you pose questions throughout the course or in a quiz at the end, make sure these are tied to those learning outcomes so you can tell from people's answers whether they have taken the learning to heart, and have the skills needed.

Keep it short by majoring on what to leave out!

Time is money, especially when it's your managers' time. The beauty of online learning is that you don't have to set aside whole days or even blocks of hours, you can do a lot in 10-20 minutes. It's also important to define how long the course should take, as this is effectively the amount of investment, in time, which you want each manager who does the course to commit to. Every minute you can shave off the course is time saved, so don't be afraid to leave stuff out, especially if it can be included as extra optional reading. Think of the main stuff they need to know as being on the 'critical learning path', the rest is optional but can add a lot of value. And when it comes to video, there's a reason most pop hits tend to come in at the three minute mark. It's enough time to make an impact without people's attention drifting. If you need to be longer, make sure there are regular 'aha' moments to keep learners interested and deriving value.

So, what are you thinking?

Now's a good time to reflect and note any ideas you have...

Chapter 5 - Turbo-charge your people's learning

Making it stick

Good course content is essential to effective learning. But it's not enough. Even if you have the very best online learning available, it's fanciful to imagine it will transform your managers' behaviour without further support to make it stick in practice as well as in theory. Coaching is what often makes the difference between learning and transformative behaviour change. But, like learning itself, coaching means different things to different people. And, like anything, it can be done badly, inefficiently and expensively. So, it's important to understand exactly what coaching is, how it works and what you want from it.

Ultimately, it's up to business leaders to lead from the front to support an environment in which managers can thrive, because every minute of upskilling is made to count. Better managers are more productive managers, so it's in everyone's interests to make the most of every bit of budget and time spent on learning. Extra help, from top-up learning and refresher courses to coaching, both external and internal, is an essential part of the mix. Coaching has the particular benefit of motivating people to strive to do better, making a personal contract with themselves.

Before going on, however, it's worth noting that even the best coaching will not make up for the negative effects of a poor working environment. The psychologist Frederick Herzberg noted in the 1960s that the factors leading to satisfaction at work and those leading to dissatisfaction were largely independent of one another. And that's a key insight that remains more relevant than ever, at a time when we are increasingly concerned with wellbeing: people can be satisfied and dissatisfied at the same time.

This is because the so-called 'hygiene factors' leading to dissatisfaction are things like salary, conditions, company values, policies and management style. Meanwhile, the 'motivation' factors leading to satisfaction have more to do with a personal sense of achievement and recognition, opportunities for advancement and growth. But in a toxic workplace where leaders have little regard for their people's wellbeing, even the best learning (motivation) will always be dragged down by an underlying dissatisfaction with life at the company (hygiene). A regular hygiene check, combined with actions if needed, can ensure people feel supported as well as keeping them motivated.

Even in the most supportive working environments, permanent behaviour change is difficult to achieve and sustain. Even after being convinced of the value of doing things differently, people often lose heart and slip back into bad old habits. It's often said it takes 21 days of persistence to form a new habit (if done often enough during that time), but studies have shown it can take much longer than that, especially for skills practised infrequently. One key factor to successful behaviour change is persistence, even when we occasionally slip up. Really good blended learning will factor in ongoing support to encourage learners' persistence. Regular, small 'chunks' of supplementary learning, beyond the core programme, can be the lowest cost and highest impact.

Coaching in the mix

Adding coaching into the mix can be particularly effective, especially for Millennials and Generation Zs, who respond well to being challenged on a one-to-one basis because it gives them a sense of purpose and achievement. Coaching also gives people the recognition they need when they're getting things right and encourages them to persevere or think more creatively when they face challenges.

Of course, managing people always involves incentives and disincentives ('carrots and sticks') and it's important to understand what those are. Someone who fails to make progress will be obvious when tested, and there may be consequences in terms of rewards and career progression opportunities. But the incentive to do well is not just financial or even a boost in status or prestige. With good learning, the real 'carrot' is seeing that all the hard work has paid off. That it works, leading to better results and greater job satisfaction. Good coaches understand this, and help people see the connection between changing their behaviour and reaping the rewards.

What do you think makes a good coach? The first thing to understand is that a good coach is not the same thing as a good management trainer. Trainers specialise in face-to-face delivery of a typically pre-formatted and sometimes structured programme. The best ones do what they do very well, and can be very entertaining, even inspirational. Some are talented amateur actors or musicians, but their role is commonly to talk to relatively passive audiences, with minimal interactivity or even questions and answers.

The next level of sophistication is a group session involving interactive role plays, but even then, there are often pre-set outcomes defined by the programme itself rather than the particular needs and preferences of the group. Nevertheless, there is still huge value in a good group session, interactive or otherwise, if it's led by a great facilitator. But session cost, expenses and duration can be prohibitive for busy managers, especially if they are geographically dispersed. Clearly having a virtual group session is an option where technology is available and reliable, but it's tough to do role plays virtually unless the participants and other attendees can see the body language.

Coaching is a different thing, entirely. It is not a coach's job to deliver content in any form. A coach is more of a listener than a talker, someone who can reflect a learner's own thoughts back to them and help them work through their challenges/opportunities themselves without prescribing solutions.

In that sense, although there are excellent professional coaches out there, as we'll go on to discuss, coaching is perhaps better seen as a role anyone can play rather than a job only for specialists. In that sense, coaching begins with a manager's own manager and peers (not to mention family and friends). For any manager, anyone and everyone around them can, and I would argue, should, be upskilled to be a mini-coach.

A positive people environment

A positive people environment is essential to make coaching efficient and effective. In the most successful and dynamic businesses I've worked with, learning is infectious rather than competitive. When people have completed a course, they don't use what they've learned to seek an edge over their colleagues, they enthusiastically share what they've learned (at no extra cost to your business). And where everyone has completed a course or even been exposed to it second-hand, there is positive reinforcement of the core messages and behaviours all supporting your business strategy. Ongoing motivation for all concerned, 'viral' learning.

A really simple way to get support when making a change in behaviour is to explain to your manager, your team and colleagues, "This is what I'm trying to do. Please support me and let's see if this works." This not only spreads the word but gives the manager an added incentive to change their behaviour and make it stick. They now have people rooting for them, and they won't want to let them down. Getting others involved and explaining goals is a brilliant way to generate positive reinforcement. This fits right in with the objectives and key results (OKRs) approach we mentioned earlier.

Nevertheless, there is certainly a role for more formal coaching, and for bringing in professionals. In that case, it's worth spending time to ensure you have the right professional for the job. Naturally, you'll want someone suitably qualified and possibly accredited by a reputable professional body, and with experience in your sector if relevant, especially as it allows the coach to occasionally be a mentor. But often word-of-mouth referrals are the best way to have confidence that a coach will really have an impact. And on that note, it's worth asking whether you already have people who could be upskilled to take on such a role. For example, a management trainer who has an aptitude for supporting learners and is willing to learn something new themselves could provide an excellent in-house solution. Those people will develop their skills and sense of achievement resulting in greater personal motivation and satisfaction, a real win-win.

In any case, good coaching requires investment but need not cost the Earth, especially with online options - 'remote coaching'. These make coaching available almost on-demand, with far more flexibility about frequency and duration. For example, you might book for 6-8 hours of coaching to take place at any time within a month in sessions of 45-60 minutes. That way everyone's time is optimised. You also have access to a global pool of coaches.

Coaching gives your managers time away from their peers to focus on their own strengths and build in other areas. It's personalised and confidential. And if combined with scenario-based online learning, learner and coach will have shared points of reference in the characters and situations set out there. For example, "Your situation is just like the one faced by Charlotte in Managing People when she had to deal with a stressed employee. How can we apply the lessons you learned from that?" This can save an incredible amount of time, as the learner will instantly know what the coach means and vice versa.

For this reason, coaches don't have to be expert practitioners in the learner's field - usually they are not. But they know the online materials, characters and scenarios, and have the requisite skills to help learners bridge the gap between competencies learned from a course and making concrete changes in practice.

Beyond coaching

Coaching is here to stay, but a word of warning - it does have its limits. Precisely because coaches are there to help people make their own decisions, they won't always get them to the right ones. But as a coach once put it to me, "Coaches can never be wrong, because they're not offering answers or opinions". Of course, if someone is really not seeing the obvious or they're stuck, their coach might be tempted to take off their coaching hat for a moment and give their opinion, but they'll always make it clear that this is not coaching, and put the hat back on again afterwards. Most would agree this is a valid approach for the right coach with the right experience. Ultimately though, it's not their responsibility to tell the manager what to do. Coaches are there to help people learn, sometimes from their own mistakes as well as their successes, often the former are more valuable.

In addition to formal and informal coaching, some learners benefit from the support of a mentor, which is something quite different. A mentor is someone who has been there and done it, someone who can draw on their own experience to give a learner advice on what to do and what not to do. Mentors do offer their opinions, and learners can benefit immensely from their expert advice. (On the downside, of course, even the wisest, most experienced mentor's opinion is sometimes wrong).

A mentoring relationship is typically more informal and organic. For example, someone might turn to an older family member who happens to be an experienced businessperson (not always from the same sector). In my case, that's my father-in-law Roger, who wrote the foreword to this book. I've been lucky to have his continued support for 25 years, and he's helped me avoid many mistakes, but also let me make some to learn from, thanks Roger.

Internal mentoring works well within a business if everyone is committed, and many companies successfully pair young managers with more experienced colleagues for regular guidance and advice. It can be especially helpful to pair people from different roles, departments and working cultures within the same sector. There's also such a thing as reverse mentoring, with younger colleagues helping their older peers get to grips with things like the emerging culture, technology and new ideas. It's all good as part of the mix, but the important thing is to understand the very different roles of coaches and mentors.

So, coaching really can turbo-charge your manager's learning, but it works best as part of a wider learning 'ecosystem' with a supportive and engaged leadership team, great course content and a variety of different forms of coaching tailored to the needs of the individuals. And, as ever, the benefits are measurable, so measure them! The best way to determine what kind of coaching gets the best results is to test learners who have worked with coaches and compare the results with those of learners who have gone without. You can also use post-coaching surveys to find out what learners think of the experience and what they might want to do differently.

You can download some example post course surveys at www.bmbb.online

Successful coaching can then be rolled out, tested again, and gradually improved again. That's the subject of the next chapter.

Turbo-charge your people's learning: Checklist

A positive learning culture starts with the Board

Business leaders bear the ultimate responsibility for creating the right environment for learning. That means ensuring both the right 'hygiene' factors in terms of governance, supportive management and consideration of wellbeing, and the right motivation factors, including access to the coaching that unlocks the potential of any other learning resources. Directors, business owners and senior managers need to be fully behind the company's learning blend and desired outcomes.

Don't expect online learning to do all the work

Even the best online courses won't get the very best results on their own. They are designed not simply to transmit information from a screen into someone's brain, but to get people thinking differently and ultimately behaving differently. The best goes way beyond knowledge to skills and gives motivation, method and confidence to make change. It's by discussing the content with peers and coaches that learners make the most of them, because they begin to see how they apply to their own working lives. So, factor in further help to reinforce learning, including opportunities for both formal and informal coaching.

Encourage viral learning

Good learning inspires people to share what they have learned. This should be encouraged as much as possible. Talking about new ideas and ways of working both reinforces them for the learners and generates knock-on benefits for their colleagues - at no extra cost! Coaching begins at an informal level with the learner's own manager and peers (who only need a little upskilling to get going), so make the most of it.

Use external or internal skilled coaches smartly and strategically

Good external coaches can be worth their weight in gold. But that doesn't mean you have to break the bank to make use of them. Online 'remote' coaching sessions are an efficient and economical option that can deliver great results. And coaching works especially well as a complement to online learning since the coach and learner alike can refer to scenarios from the learning and apply the lessons to real-life challenges and opportunities.

Understand the role of mentors

Mentors are not the same as coaches, but they can also play an invaluable role. They bring experience and wisdom to the learner, so mentoring relationships can be an excellent supplement to more conventional learning and coaching. Just don't confuse the two!

Keep measuring the results!

Not all coaching will be equally effective, and not all provides value for money. So, always measure the results of coaching to establish what works and what does not, use post-coaching surveys to get learners' perspectives, and refine your future coaching approach based on your findings.

So, what are you thinking?

Now's a good time to reflect and note any ideas you have...

Chapter 6 - Knowing it's working

Measuring your blend

The right blend of learning and coaching should make a tangible difference to your business. But if you are going to demonstrate value for money and identify which elements of learning are most and least effective, you need to be able to measure the impact they are having.

Naturally, the Board will want to see a return on investment, as should all good L&D teams, but that's only one measure for effective learning. Return on investment is fiscal and numerical. It involves hard numbers, the sum invested, the savings achieved, or the profits yielded. The downside is that financial numbers don't necessarily tell the whole story when it comes to management. Upskilling your managers should lead to better performance from the whole team, which should ultimately result in positive business outcomes that show up at the bottom line, but there are so many other variables. Simply looking at return on investment is only part of the picture.

Consider another example: a sports team can invest in excellent coaching, but there is no guarantee that it will directly result in more wins, at least not straight away, it might be next season or beyond. Maybe you have a run of bad luck or injury, but if you can see that the players are getting fitter, faster and more skilful, you know the investment is still worthwhile and likely to lead to better results sooner or later. On the other hand, a few lucky wins should not be allowed to obscure the fact that overall performance is declining. Of course, it's often said you make your own luck, and while business leaders always seek to manage external and internal risk, it's important to be able to isolate and measure the effects of a specific learning programme or approach as much as possible.

This is why we increasingly talk not just about return on investment but return on expectation. Is your learning and development helping align your managers with your values and strategy, by giving them the skills they need in a way that suits their style and generation? If so, it's doing what you asked of it, and unless you have reason to doubt the strategy, you should stick with it. If not, you need to reconsider what you're doing regardless of short-term results.

What you need to be able to measure is your managers' ability to apply the right knowledge and skills in particular situations. You can't follow them around for the whole working day monitoring their every decision, but you can at least test that they understand the right thing to do in any given situation. Referring back to Managing People as an example, each episode focuses on a different aspect of real-world management: Preparation, Wellbeing, Recruitment, Induction, Coaching & Performance Management, Appraisals and Managing Talent, and assesses a manager's grasp of the competencies required, helping them know the right thing to do.

Skills check

And once your managers are making real progress, we can take a close-up look at more detailed assessment, using a similar approach to the Quick Skills Check that we looked at earlier to do the initial assessment. For each of Managing People's seven episodes, there is a Mastery Check. Each one asks learners 10 questions based on the content of the relevant episode. As with the course itself, the idea is to be as practical as possible, by focusing on how skills and behaviours manifest themselves in real-life situations. This is not just about testing knowledge; it's about assessing how a manager would behave. If these are done a few days after completing the learning and coaching, they give a measure of what's changed and beginning to be put into practice. The questions start with underpinning knowledge and associated skills, then move to sophisticated scenarios demanding multiple skills.

Each scenario is then mapped to the behaviours you need your managers to have, which are grouped into competencies (you can download our set here *www.bmbb.online*.) Each answer is weighted according to how much the question verifies that learners are demonstrating particular behaviours and using their skills appropriately.

 Managing People - Mastery Check

Question

A month ago you recruited a new team leader. For the first few weeks they were extremely enthusiastic and engaged with the team and their training. Last week they appeared less enthusiastic, although when you asked them how it was going, they didn't raise any concerns.

Your other team leader has also mentioned to you that they don't think they're the right person for the job. When probed, they said they didn't think they were picking up tasks quickly enough when they were training them and were asking too many questions. On the other hand, several team members who will be working for them have come up to you and mentioned how lovely they are and looking forward to working for them.

You are starting to be a little concerned.

What combination of the below actions should you be taking prior to their next review?

(A) Check what training has been completed against their induction plan

(B) Ask the existing team leader for some specific examples that you can discuss with the new team leader

(C) Work alongside the new team leader and observe them in action

(D) Take a look at any relevant customer feedback/financial reports to see if any patterns exist

(E) Speak to the new team leader informally about them not seeming themselves

(F) Keep your distance from the new team leader as this needs to be talked about formally during the review

- ○ Answers A, C and D
- ● Answers B and F
- ○ Answers A, C, D and E
- ○ Answers B, C, D, and F

Crucially, each question tests specific behaviours associated with each competency group. For example, good communication behaviours include 'Adapts style in communication to match the audience' and 'Knows how and when to listen', while good planning and organising behaviours include 'Sets stretching, realistic targets and goals for self and others within the team' and 'Knows what to refer upwards, when and how'. For each question, the weight per competency is the total of the weighting for each behaviour, scored from 1 to 5 (showing minimal to strong evidence of that behaviour).

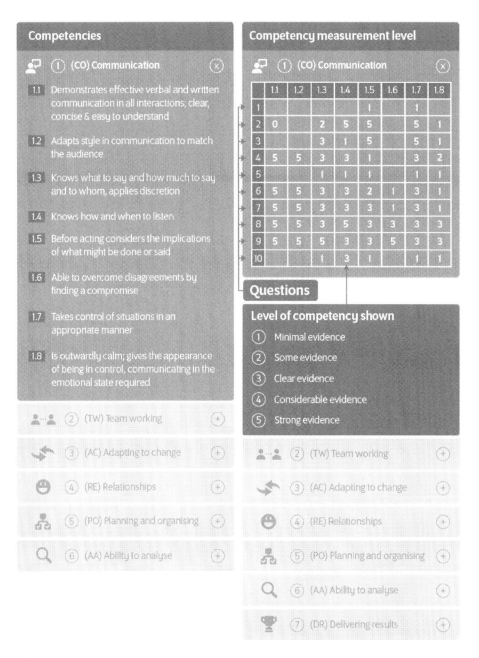

So, for example, giving the best answer for one question might demonstrate good communication skills and team working skills but reveal little about the ability to analyse and nothing about the other competencies (adapting to change, relationships, planning and organising or delivering results). Another question might indicate much about communication, nothing about the others, but a lot about adapting to change skills and planning and organising. Each question, therefore, gives a much more precise indication of the learner's strengths or areas for improvement.

The results after completing all 70 questions in all seven Mastery Checks are far more powerful than a simple score based on whether someone gets each question right or wrong, adding up to just a pass or fail. Instead, each learner is given an overall score for each competency in the form of a percentage. If someone's score is low, you can then dig into the data to identify which questions are causing issues, and the behaviours they need to work on. Question-level analysis, therefore, allows for much more targeted and efficient coaching and personalised management development.

In fact, it's worth emphasising here that the Mastery Check, and anything like it that you put together yourself, is meant to be used as a tool as part of the learning and coaching process, not as purely a stand-alone assessment. Unlike a Quick Skills Check, the point is not to check where your managers are before they upskill, but to identify areas for improvement to get them to the next level. They must be challenging, if lots of people are getting 100%, the questions are too easy (or you have some amazing managers, so celebrate). Normally 50-70% should be considered a 'pass', and then you can focus on the 30-50% the manager is not doing as well as you need them to and build on where they are.

Of course, it's also possible to calculate an aggregate team score for each competency, which is invaluable when planning further learning for the whole team. And better still, you can compare scores across a team and identify any unevenness. From there, you can focus on levelling the team up so everyone meets an acceptable standard. This ensures the whole team is benefitting from the learning, which means it's far more likely to have positive outcomes for the business. Indeed, you can also break down results by other demographics to see if colleagues in different locations/departments, or those playing different roles, are at different levels so you can really target support. All this information is useful, not only in assessing the efficacy of your company's core learning but also in planning future supplementary learning and updating online content. You'll get a better picture to help you make better decisions.

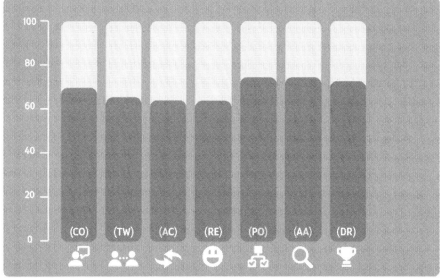

ID PN6949	Individual Competency Analysis								
		CO	TW	AC	RE	PO	AA	DR	
Question	Answers	1	2	3	4	5	6	7	
1	Correct	2	22	0	8	10	18	5	
2	Wrong	0	0	0	0	0	0	0	
3	Correct	15	7	18	12	18	16	5	
4	Correct	22	6	3	12	3	11	7	
5	Wrong	0	0	0	0	0	0	0	
6	Correct	23	12	3	14	2	6	10	
7	Correct	24	12	11	9	8	11	5	
8	Wrong	0	0	0	0	0	0	0	
9	Correct	32	13	8	17	11	6	12	
10	Correct	7	13	8	18	8	17	5	
Total	545	125	85	51	90	60	85	49	Overall
Level		69%	65%	63%	63%	76%	75%	73%	69%

Competencies key

(CO) Communication   (TW) Team working   (AC) Adapting to change   (RE) Relationships

(PO) Planning and organising   (AA) Ability to analyse   (DR) Delivering results

If the Mastery Check sounds complicated, it is, and it isn't. It takes skill and an investment in time to create and refine (think 20 revisions at least). It's certainly sophisticated and powerful, but once you have a comprehensive set of weighted questions, the assessment is very easy to use, and the data can be automatically crunched, analysed and put into easy to read formats so you can compare progress over time. The hard part is coming up with the questions in the first place, but then if it were easy, everyone would be doing it!

Nevertheless, the principles behind all this are relatively simple. One way or another, you need to be able to measure not simply the number of courses completed, quizzes passed, or even short-term business outcomes, but the extent to which your people are developing their ability to apply the right knowledge and skills in particular situations, repeatedly. And you need to test before and after each element of learning, from online learning to coaching and mentoring, to identify which are having an impact - ideally by testing against a control group that has not had one or more elements.

Don't limit yourself

But you don't have to limit yourself to one form of measurement. Using more will give you a fuller picture, but choose wisely or you'll end up with 'analysis paralysis', drowning in data. Not all data is useful, and too much is a distraction from what really matters rather than being an added benefit.

There is also a place for post-course and post-coaching surveys, if they are quick, well thought out and used smartly. We're all familiar with the feedback forms used after traditional training courses. Cynics call them 'happy sheets' since they tick the boxes necessary to keep everyone happy (especially those signing off the budgets), but are then often consigned to a folder (digital or physical) never to be seen again! Good surveys should make life easier, not soak up time in deriving unhelpful and uninformative information. They also aren't limited to courses and engagement, they can look at topics that have been focused on in the management programme, such as wellbeing.

The questions can be tailored to whatever you want to know, but typically they will ask learners whether they learned skills they could use, enjoyed the course, whether they would like to do more of the same kind, and whether they feel they've benefitted from it. You can also ask more technical questions like whether they feel the course was the right length or level of difficulty, and whether they completed it at work or at home. If the latter, this might show keenness, or suggest their manager is not as supportive as they could be, which is a learning culture issue, so the data must be interpreted intelligently.

You can download an example business benefit wellbeing survey at *www.bmbb.online*

Including space for comments is a good way to solicit more qualitative feedback at best. Such comments are like a live social media feed about the company's learning, but only if they are reviewed as frequently as you would look on social media. Don't leave it a few weeks, months or years! You can then analyse them and look for trends by creating 'word clouds'. The comments you'll get can be really enlightening, enabling L&D and management teams alike to spot patterns and identify new ideas that would never have emerged otherwise. It's easier to find 100 small ideas from managers (and their team) that improve things by 1% than one huge idea to give a 100% improvement.

If you have feedback surveys from a variety of elements of learning - articles, documents, online, face-to-face, coaching, etc., you can compare them to gauge which are working better than others. Of course, surveys gather subjective impressions rather than demonstrating an objective impact, but these are handy as a supplement to the consistent and objective data that comes from something like a Mastery Check.

In fact, this kind of information is especially useful as a supplement to more ambiguous data. Take staff retention rates. These have been one of the key metrics for judging the performance of managers and HR departments. But high turnover of staff is not always something managers can control. Certainly, they can unwittingly encourage it - it's often said that, "You don't leave a company, you leave a manager", but increasingly it's happening anyway. Millennials are much less likely than previous generations to commit to a company for the long term, so I would argue that the challenge for managers is to make the most of them while they're there, especially by making sure they learn fast and have an immediate impact.

Rather than simply looking at churn, it's helpful to have something like exit interviews. They can be very effective if done in two stages, one as they leave and another later digitally (via email or other platform) to gather a more honest and open opinion they may have been unhappy to give when interviewed. This will help gauge whether people leave because they are unhappy with the management or working environment, or whether they've had a successful and positive time at the company, were invested in and felt valued, but simply felt like moving on to progress. If it's the latter, their managers are doing good work. You can use something like a Net Promoter score to gauge whether people who move on are going to be talking the company up or down. Word spreads, and a good employer brand or reputation, created with ex-employees saying great things verbally and online, will make it far easier to replace team members who have left and attract more. So, subjective impressions are important and should be captured whenever possible to measure your attractiveness rating. You can even use them to identify small changes in what you offer that could make a big difference, especially for managers, or those aspiring to be managers who have potential.

Used in combination, Mastery Checks and feedback surveys are an excellent way to get a detailed and granular sense of the impact learning is having. But, of course, there's another consideration - cost, in time as well as money. An online course might achieve only 80-90% of the expected value that would be achieved from a great day-long workshop, but if it's a fraction of the cost, that might be a very good reason to opt for it! Good online learning before classroom learning is also likely to optimise the impact, so a blend of the two will often offer the best of both worlds financially as well as in terms of effectiveness.

Whatever you choose to spend money on, reliable measurement is the key to ensuring learning is not just cost-effective but delivers value and benefit. 'Buy right, or buy twice', assuming you've some budget left. And repetition and reiteration are the key to progression, as we'll discuss in the next chapter.

Knowing it's working: Checklist

Think return on expectation, not just investment

The purpose of learning is to give your managers the skills they need to do their jobs better and deliver your business strategy in line with your values. Realising that goal should be the measure of success, alongside any cost saving from improving your approach and efficiency. If the Board does not get this, it's up to HR to push back and make the case!

Focus on competencies and behaviours, not just knowledge

It's easy to test people for knowledge of facts and soundbites. The real challenge is to measure their ability to put that knowledge into practice in real-life. Do they have the competencies and behaviours they need? If you're not measuring that, you're working in the dark!

Gather meaningful data and learn from it

The more detailed the data you can get about your people's competencies, the better. Passing or failing an old-fashioned, knowledge-based test tells you very little about whether progress is being made and where. Once you've established learners' strengths and areas for improvement, you can tweak their learning and coaching accordingly both at individual and team level. HR teams should regularly share the data analysis and impact with the business leaders to demonstrate progress and sustain buy-in. The flipside is that business leaders should be demanding to see (the right) data.

Use the data to predict outcomes and improve the process

Once you're in the habit of measuring before and after each learning element, you should be able to predict the expected outcomes. This is more like looking through the front windscreen than the rear-view mirror. Post-learning measurement is then a case of confirming return on expectation so you can adjust accordingly if the results are not as expected. This is about taking control of the process so you can gradually improve it rather than learning from scratch what works and what does not. It's an iterative process, expect and plan for continual investment in improvements. In content, structure and approach, keep tweaking until it's 'good enough'.

Use qualitative surveys too

Surveys are a useful way to establish whether people are engaged with their learning, and which elements are benefitting them most. Gather as much feedback as you can, but in a format that's efficient to get value from quickly and use it both to gauge the success of the learning and to make enhancements.

Measure coaching as well as courses

If you're spending money on it, measure it! Coaching is often an excellent way to turbo-charge your manager's learning, but measuring its impact by testing against a control group is the best way to demonstrate value for money, or to identify what could work better and adjust accordingly. Scrap the paper and spreadsheets, too cumbersome costly and slow, your managers are important, invest in them. Always survey the managers online, it's quick and easy.

Beware of dubious metrics

It's not only return on investment that can fail to tell the whole story. Boards are used to judging HR on retention rates, but these are not the whole picture. Great feedback from people moving on is also valuable. In general, just because you have numbers it does not mean they are meaningful or useful ('vanity statistics'). So, think carefully about exactly what you want to measure and make sure that it's aligned with what the numbers are revealing is happening, or not as the case may be.

So, what are you thinking?

Now's a good time to reflect and note any ideas you have...

Chapter 7 - What happens next?

Make it a habit

Everything we've covered so far is tried and tested. It works if done well, and will make a positive difference to your business. But it's more of a fitness regime than a one-off spa treatment. To be effective, it must become a habit. So, after one round of learning, coaching and measuring progress, you need to be thinking about the next one, and weaving this approach into everything you do.

'Annual' appraisals are increasingly less relevant as they're too infrequent - the same can be true of management development. Measure, develop, assess, review, repeat should take place on a three-to-six-month cycle, in some cases more frequently. This allows for constant improvement and adjustment in line with the needs of the business. People also prefer it, especially (but not exclusively) Millennials and Generation Zs. They want to feel that they're making progress and benefitting from proactive management and career development. They value a regular opportunity to raise and discuss any frustrations and they appreciate constant feedback. The objectives and key results (OKRs) approach has conversations, feedback and recognition (CFR) sessions at its core. Any feedback is good but especially when it's positive, and if their learning is working as it should be, it will be!

Cyclical upskilling and assessment also provide opportunities to develop the learning itself, and keep the Board appraised of how things are going. Rather than receiving annual reports and requests for more funding, they benefit from a real-time overview of what's being spent and how learning is meeting expectations, in terms of upskilling the company's managers. The shocking truth is that it's often possible to achieve more with less than is currently being spent. Indeed, constant and smart measurement of outcomes also reveals whether learning is providing value for money. Something that works well but costs the Earth should perhaps be dropped in favour of a cheaper but 'good enough' alternative. It's always worth considering the possibility that some forms of support, while effective, are just not worth the cost or effort. And of course, something that exceeds expectations for little cost should be rolled out more fully. Having the data puts these options at your fingertips. In our digital age, the successful commercial media platforms are those that measure the popularity of everything they put out, drop their duds and produce more of what people like. You can do the same, though the metric is improved competencies rather than more viewers.

Aligning with your business

We started by talking about the importance of aligning learning with your business strategy, and as that strategy changes, so too should your learning. Once defined, the competencies your managers need are unlikely to change much, but the way they need to be applied will be different at different times. The ability to measure those competencies means you can instantly identify any shortfall in the level of the specific behaviours that are required at any given time and act fast. Otherwise, it provides reassurance that all your managers have the skills they need to thrive, and you can take a lighter touch to maintaining and refreshing those competencies for your existing managers.

Once you have a successful learning culture up and running, and once all your managers have the right, balanced set of demonstrable skills, you can also experiment with supplementary forms of learning to help 'top up' your people's knowledge. Why not produce short films to share ideas and expertise on a more ad-hoc basis? Imagine a cache of TED-style talks tailored to your business' own needs. Even a three minute clip can get people thinking differently, and of course you can add that all-important scenario-based assessment to make sure they've got it, accept it and help it stick. And best of all, you can measure the results and apply the lessons to what you do next.

Whatever you do, measure it. Learn what's working and what's not and use that information to ensure your learning remains both effective and fully aligned with your business strategy. You'll have the data to make every bit of budget and every minute count. Use it.

What happens next? Checklist

Just one this time: make better learning and constant improvement a habit. A three-to-six-month cycle of learning, coaching and measuring will keep your learning relevant, cost-effective and cutting edge. And crucially, an ongoing, strategic approach to learning will keep the Board and HR working in unison and harmony (well, most of the time) and that means better managers and equals a better business.

So, what are you thinking?

Now's a good time to reflect and note any ideas you have...

Conclusion

So, now you've seen how upskilled managers and their teams can make a real difference to how a business performs. You've seen how truly measuring managers' competencies is the key to bridging the gap between where they are now and where you need them to be. And you've found out how a strategic blend of different kinds of learning can not only give them the knowledge they need, but also translate that knowledge into practical skills and ultimately behaviour change that resonates through your business, often reducing costs in the process.

Now, if you've skipped here for a quick summary of what this book is about and whether it's worth your time, the paragraph above just about sums up why I wrote it. But if I could have summarised the content in a few bullet points, I'd have done so, saving my time as well as yours!

If you have read through the whole thing, or at least read enough to be convinced there's something in this, I have a question for you, "What are you going to do about it?" Let's be practical. You're not going to transform your managers overnight. But what positive steps can you take, starting right now, that will make a real difference?

If you're a CEO, business owner or senior manager, it might be taking this book to your learning and development (L&D) team and starting a conversation about how you can apply some of these ideas to your business. If you're in L&D, you might be thinking how your relationship with the Board should change and how little innovations could make a big difference. This book gives you what you need to get the backing of decision makers at CEO or Board level. If you start measuring competencies linked to business goals, you can both show the need for better learning, and begin to demonstrate the results.

Once decision makers and L&D are aligned, things really start to happen. That might mean a comprehensive overhaul of your business' learning strategy. The principles set out above will help ensure you make the very best of it. But, frankly, anything you do along the lines I've suggested, however small, will make a difference. Even more frankly, doing nothing is not an option. And making plans for next year is just another way of doing nothing!

Equally though, there's no point being so ambitious that you can't possibly live up to your stated goals. And there's no point reinventing the wheel if stuff is out there and ready to go. So, think about what you can take from what you've read and put it into action now. If you don't, your competitors will.

In many cases, it's measurement that's the real game changer. It's what takes you from scrabbling in the dark and hoping, to really taking control of your managers' learning. From there, you're in a position to design personalised learning tailored to their needs. And as we've seen, little and often is much better than periodic training or away days, especially for the Millennials and Generation Zs.

This way, you can also assess how effective particular elements of learning are and adapt accordingly. If online learning is not sticking, what about coaching or mentoring to turbo-charge the process? Are people hitting a plateau? What kind of supplementary learning might make a difference? Bear in mind that you may have untapped resources within your business. Trainers who could be upskilled to be coaches, for example. If not, external support is always available, and online options mean it could be less expensive than you think.

The key is to keep finding that one thing that will help your managers keep improving, even in small increments. It all adds up, so keep going around the loop:

- Define what you need your managers to be able to do

- Assess current ability level

- Create a learning programme

- Provide knowledge and convert to skills

- Enable further support to entrench behaviour change

- Assess ability level

- Review, revise, repeat

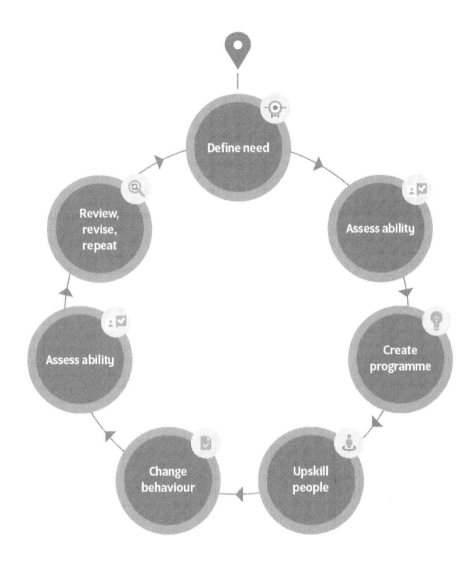

Once you've made a start, you'll begin to see results. And once you see the possibilities, you won't want to stop. Better managers really do make for better businesses, and the power to unleash the potential of your managers is in your hands - literally! I hope you'll find this book helpful, but of course it's up to you to put these ideas into practice. As we've seen, repetition is key, so do come back to the book for a refresher whenever you need to, that's a good learning approach. You'll find these ideas make more sense the more you apply them, as will your managers. So good luck and get going today!

Thank you to...

This book is no different to most others in that it wouldn't have happened or have been half as good without a wonderful set of people to review, comment and give honest opinions. So, thank you to Caroline, Dolan, Jillian, Dave, Lou, John, Rupert, Victoria, Geoff, Lawrence, Les, Sue and of course Roger for your wonderful help, and thank you to everyone I've learned things from over the years.

A little bonus - Florence

Just like on some albums where you get a bonus track at the end. I thought a bonus book would be good. I wrote '**Sausage Factory - A story about Florence**' to be a little provocative.

Sausage Factory is a business just like many others, competing in an ever more challenging environment. The story is about it, and how it develops managers like Florence. You'll like Florence.

If it makes you smile and even laugh out loud that's great. I do hope you don't recognise too much of the story from what happens at your organisation, but above all, I hope it gives you a little nudge to think about where things might be a little better.

Sausage Factory

A story about Florence

Better Managers, Better Business

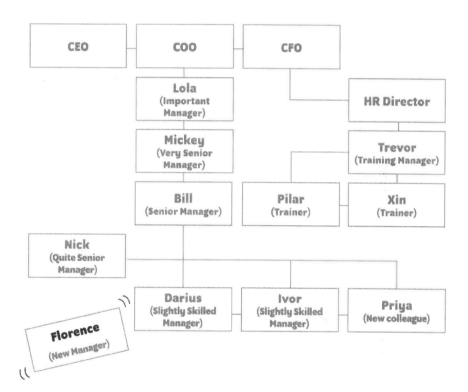

New job, new horizons

Florence is excited about her new job as a manager at Sausage Factory. She's young, idealistic and super ambitious. She knows she has a lot to learn, but she's looking forward to learning from the best. Before she was due to start, she was sent a video link to watch the CEO tell her inspirational story about how she'd started working in the industry straight out of school and risen to the top. Apparently, she'd had a fantastic coach to guide her progress. "And that's how I realised that cultivating people is key to the success of any business," she said. She certainly sounded more convincing than the other executive in the video, who said something similar, but made it sound like he was reading from an inspirational poster with a cheesy quote pasted over a photo of a sunrise.

Still, Florence has been assured that Sausage Factory has a learning and development department that is second to none. Its trainers have degrees in helping young professionals like Florence become better managers. They are members of all the recognised people development bodies. She knows this because it says so on their LinkedIn profiles. With their help, there will be nothing to stop Florence becoming the best manager she can be.

The Board is excited about Florence. She is just the kind of 'bright young thing' Sausage Factory needs to grow and reach the next level. The Board is made up of clever men and women whose job it is to make sure the company succeeds.

They have a strategy to do just that, and according to that strategy, people are what make businesses better - people like Florence. That's why they've invested lots of money in the learning and development department. They believe it will give Sausage Factory a competitive advantage. This is strange, because they don't actually have any idea what the learning and development department does, or whether it provides value for money.

Training away day: the countdown

Florence is especially excited about the upcoming Training Away Day, which is actually two whole days of high-level learning and development. Florence can't wait. In fact, she's so enthusiastic that she's reached out to Pilar, the trainer in charge, to ask what she can do to prepare. Florence loves learning new stuff.

The funny thing is, that while Pilar is very active on LinkedIn and Twitter, she has not replied to any of Florence's emails or returned her calls. Florence's senior manager, Bill, says Pilar must be very busy. Bill's been at Sausage Factory for longer than most. He says HR people are famously busy. He says, if they had time to sit around replying to emails and returning calls, people would start to think they had nothing better to do. Bill has a way of laughing without really smiling.

Pilar is stressed. Pilar is always stressed. She has 463 unread emails in her inbox. Her boss, Trevor, says anyone with less than 500 unread emails is a lightweight. Pilar knows he should say fewer than 500, not less, but who is she to question his wisdom? Unlike Pilar and most of her colleagues, Trevor has operational experience. He spent several years managing a series of Sausage Factory branches which all closed before it was decided that his talents would be better used in training others.

It was Trevor who booked the venue for the Training Away Day. It's a state-of-the-art conference centre cum-budget hotel, nestled cosily in the midst of the motorway interchange just outside town. He has a contact there who got him a 'sweet deal', though it won't actually cost the company any less than a similar event last year. When it comes to the budget, Trevor's motto is 'use it or lose it!' The sweet deal seems to involve an extra night away from the family for Trevor. Trevor has a way of winking that makes everyone feel uncomfortable.

Pilar is looking at her emails. She opens one from IT because it has a little flag on it to show that it's urgent. They are unable to help with a guest speaker's request for IT support for his presentation. Since the event is outside company premises, that would involve a breach of security. They suggest she asks the venue for help. Pilar opens another urgent email from an area manager who says he can't afford to release his team for the Training Away Day. Most of the other managers have been on it before and have said they will make it optional for their people.

Sometimes Pilar feels like the rest of the business doesn't really value what the learning and development team does. She has brought this up with Trevor and suggested raising it with the Board, especially because in recent memos, they've said they value learning and development very much. It's at the heart of their strategy. Pilar doesn't understand at all. But Trevor tells her not to worry about it. His other favourite motto is, 'don't rock the boat'.

Pilar has lots of other urgent emails, but she doesn't feel like opening them. She is even more stressed about the Training Away Day and it's very soon now. Pilar feels like crying.

The big day(s)

Florence arrives at the conference centre bright and early on the morning of Day One of the Training Away Day. She is the first to arrive! When the learning and development team arrive a little later, Florence is given a welcome pack containing the agenda, some hotel stationery and a four-page feedback booklet. The feedback booklet is labelled 'Sausage Factory Training Away Day 2016'. It is 2019.

Slowly, some more colleagues begin to arrive, and Florence recognises Priya and Nick. "Hello, Priya! Hello, Nick!" Priya and Nick say hello. They want to know where the coffee is.

The Training Away Day is opened by Pilar. She thanks everyone for coming and says she hopes everyone is ready to learn. She says it in a way that suggests she doesn't expect them to be ready to learn. Pilar seems tired.

She introduces the first speaker, her colleague Xin, who is a very experienced trainer. She clearly got some of her experience at another company, because her second slide has their logo in the corner. Most people don't notice, because they are looking at their phones.

After about 45 minutes, Xin makes a joke about how her colleagues don't seem to have woken up yet. "Don't worry", she says, "it's time for a breakout session. That'll get us all going." She divides the room into groups and asks them to brainstorm a crisis scenario on big sheets of paper.

Xin doesn't want to unduly influence people's thinking, so she steps outside for a vape. Trevor is already there smoking a real cigarette. Trevor is old school. Trevor and Xin are old friends.

Trevor finds it easier to work with people who understand how things work, and over the years he has built up a network of trusted HR people in and outside the business. Seasoned people trainers who can put on a good show, tell jokes and teach everyone the cardinal rules of management. The cardinal rules of management have not changed since the beginning of time, so why should training techniques?

He tells Xin he gets frustrated when colleagues like Pilar suggest doing things differently, but the good news is that Pilar is coming around to his way of seeing things. Tried and tested ways. The way everyone else does it. "If it ain't broke," he says, and Xin joins in to finish yet another favourite motto: "don't fix it!"

Breakout

Florence is pleased to be in the same group as Priya and Nick. She asks them how they think the change management scenario they've been asked to consider relates to Sausage Factory's business strategy. Priya and Nick laugh.

Florence is trying to apply the competencies she's read about to the situation. Priya and Nick look at Florence as if she is a sweet little bunny. Florence is a bit annoyed. Priya explains that it doesn't matter what they write on their big sheet of paper because nobody will read it anyway.

Florence says, "wasting all that paper can't be very good for the planet." "Good point", says Nick, looking at his phone.

Florence looks again at the change management scenario outlined in the handout. Even as a brand-new manager, she can see that it's not very realistic, and the answers are obvious (even with the spelling mistakes). She has made copious notes on her own pad, but she can't imagine how they are going to help her in the real world. 'Handle the situation sensitively and communicate clearly,' she has written. That's a no brainer, but what would it mean in practice? That would depend on the situation, and the one in the scenario is too vague to provide any real challenge.

If there are no questions...

In the next session, Trevor is talking about approaches to business development. Florence has a question. She puts her hand up. "The toilet's that way," Trevor says, pointing at the exit. Trevor doesn't like questions. Questions are unpredictable. What if he doesn't have the answer? But Florence's hand is still up. "All right. What's your question?" he says.

Florence's question is about a real-life situation. Trevor doesn't know the answer, but he can't let on. He nods sagely as if he does know the answer. "Who'd like to answer that?" he asks. Most people look at the floor, but Darius puts his hand up. Darius is good looking and knows it. He enjoys the spotlight. "I'll tell you what I'd do," he says. What he goes on to say sounds to Florence like a terrible idea. She's not even sure it would be legal.

"Well, there you go then," says Trevor. For the rest of the day, the only people to speak up from the floor are attention seekers like Darius. When they share their mad ideas, everyone looks at Florence like it's her fault.

By the end of the day, Florence is more than a bit fed up. She doesn't feel like she's learned anything, except that people don't seem to take training very seriously. Even the guest speaker fell a bit flat, having complained she didn't have the IT setup she'd expected and couldn't show the funny video she'd got from a TV series. That must have been the highlight of her talk, because without it she didn't seem to have anything to say. Florence asks her colleagues if it's always like this. "Pretty much", they say. She wonders if things are like this at other companies.

Online: the future that failed?

Then someone points out that they had online training last year, and everyone laughs. It was supposed to save lots of time and money and make the world a better place.

Apparently, someone had just clicked through all the questions guessing the answers until they got them right, and then stuck all the answers online. The online training had been Pilar's idea, but she hadn't really had the time or training to do it properly, and it had ended up being a complete flop. That was partly because the system the supplier had delivered wasn't quite what Pilar had been sold by the salesperson.

The demo had looked easy and intuitive. What they ended up with was much more technically demanding and time consuming, so Pilar had ended up using only the most basic bits and began to realise how hard it is to produce good courses.

"You've paid for NASA spaceflight software and got Nintendo!" Trevor had said. Trevor was very witty. He was also glad to see the online training fail. That kind of thing called for skills and creativity, which he and his network didn't have. If it took off, they'd be expected to be much more responsive and knowledgeable, more like coaches or mentors than trainers.

Then they'd be out of a job, and who'd feed their families?

Who needs data? We've got happy sheets

It was just as well the Board hadn't asked for proof that they were getting value for money from the online system. If Pilar ever left – which was something she daydreamed about a lot – her replacement would probably take one look at the mess she'd made of the system and order a new one from scratch, from an even better salesperson. And of course, they wouldn't have time to evaluate it fully, because, like Pilar, they would be very busy.

Pilar hadn't felt like proposing new ideas since the failed online experiment, even though she had a lot.

There is dinner and drinks at the end of Day One, but Pilar doesn't feel like going. Florence feels awkward because so many people are whispering about 'office-politics'. Her colleagues don't seem to like each other very much. She decides to have an early night to escape the toxic atmosphere. She's not the only one. Trevor and Xin are standing at the bar having a drink as they watch their colleagues slowly melt away. "I don't understand the youth," says Trevor. "They'd rather talk to each other online than over a drink!"

Day Two of the Training Away Day goes much like Day One, except that not everyone has stuck around. Pilar's main priority is to make sure everyone completes the feedback.

Trevor calls these 'happy sheets'. He says positive feedback is how they'll measure the success of the Training Away Day so, as long as colleagues are kind enough to tick the 'Very satisfied' box for each question, everyone will be happy.

Last year, Pilar had questioned whether this was scientific enough. Trevor had explained that they would present the results in the form of percentages. You can't get any more scientific than that! If the Board asked for anything more substantial, and especially if they brought up the question of 'return on investment', it was important to be clear that 'we don't do data'.

HR is more an art than a science anyway, he explained. You only look silly if you try to convey the magic of learning and development in the form of data. Except for percentages. Percentages are good.

So, Pilar dutifully gathers up the completed happy sheets at the end of the day. "No one really listens to us anyway," a slightly melancholy Trevor says to Xin as they watch. "We're busy enough just getting on with things", Xin adds, looking anxiously at her email inbox on her phone.

Unsettled dreams

Florence has ticked the 'Very satisfied' box for each question on her feedback sheets. Everyone else did, so it would have seemed rude to do anything else. Actually, Ivor had ticked the 'Not satisfied at all' boxes. Ivor had been bad tempered since the morning on Day One.

By the end of Day Two, Priya pointed out that he looked like a grumpy pug dog. He said the whole Training Away Day, both of them, was a waste of time and taught him nothing. "There's always one," Pilar had said. Truth be told, Florence thinks Ivor has a point. As she hands her feedback to Pilar, she wonders if there's a better way of doing learning and development. There must be a better way.

That night, Florence dreams about leaving Sausage Factory and finding a more supportive employer with a real purpose and commitment to invest in its managers and people. She dreams up a company called Made for Millennials, which doesn't feel like a hangover from the last century. At Made for Millennials, learning and development is integrated with the business strategy and the latest thinking. It's measured to make sure it's actually benefitting all managers and providing value for money. What a lovely dream!

But then Florence wakes up. Back to Sausage Factory! She thinks about some of her friends, who have moved jobs more than once since starting work. She's beginning to think she might do the same. But she's only been at Sausage Factory a few weeks, and she surely has so much to learn. The main thing she has learned so far is that 'learning' and 'training' are not the same thing.

When Florence returns to work the next day, Bill calls and asks how the Training Away Day went. She says it was fine. Bill asks what she will do differently now she has the benefit of two days' learning and development. Florence is stumped. Bill laughs, and even on the phone, she can tell it's the laugh where he doesn't smile. Florence is determined to learn what she can from Bill, but he's not what anyone would call a coach, let alone a mentor.

Florence wishes she had a great coach. Someone who understood her and wanted to help her achieve her potential, even a little bit. And she wishes Sausage Factory would make more of an effort to support her by providing modern, relevant and personalised learning. She wants professional development based on what the business needs to achieve, rather than explaining lots of outdated management theories.

Perhaps that way, they could even achieve more while spending less. Isn't that the sort of thing the Board was supposed to be making happen?

Maybe she should write them a note to tell them about Made for Millennials. If Made for Millennials were a real company, it would have a serious competitive advantage. Sausage Factory would be in trouble.

Florence can't help thinking she won't be at Sausage Factory for much longer. She knows there's better out there. She wants to be part of a team of people like her, who have a purpose.

A bit about the author

Pete Fullard is the forward-thinking CEO of Upskill People, the online learning company that helps people shine. He is rightly proud of what the company has achieved since he founded it in 1995 to produce engaging courses that actually work. The learning and development sector has changed a great deal in that time, and Pete has always been at the forefront of that change. The enduring principle behind the company is that if businesses are going to pay good money to upskill their people, the outcomes should be measurable.

While Pete is very much an ideas man, he really gets business and people: what motivates him is working with ambitious people of all ages and backgrounds, helping them achieve their potential. More than a manager, he is a natural mentor, and his energy and enthusiasm are infectious, even after more than 25 years! He is driven to get things done quickly and determined to do them the right way, with an eye on not just profit, but also people and the planet.

Pete will work through lots of alternatives if that's what's needed to get things just right. He has a knack of focusing on the positive in any situation and identifying ways to tackle challenges as well as looking for opportunities. His key talent is understanding, innovating and delivering impactful ways of doing things. He also uses his experience to get creative as a non-executive director helping other organisations do things better. Invariably, that involves measuring outcomes!

Printed in Poland
by Amazon Fulfillment
Poland Sp. z o.o., Wrocław

64756286R00069